PORT DINORWIC

By the same author

Bridges and Ferries

Arian – the Story of Money and Banking in Wales

Felinheli – A personal history of the Port of Dinorwic

Bless 'Em All – aspects of the War in North-West Wales, 1939–45

Curiouser and Curiouser – Oddities in North-West Wales

Sailing the Strait – aspects of Port Dinorwic and the Menai Strait

Dinorwic – the Llanberis Slate Quarry, 1780–1969

Anglesey & Gwynedd the War Years, 1939–45

Crossing the Menai, an illustrated history of the ferries and bridges of the Menai Strait

PORT DINORWIC
AN ILLUSTRATED HISTORY

REG CHAMBERS JONES

bridge
books

Port Dinorwic an illustrated history
First published in Wales in 2013
by Bridge Books
61 Park Avenue
WREXHAM
LL12 7AW

www.bridgebooks.co.uk

ISBN 978-1-84494-092-9

A CIP entry for this book is available from the British Library

Printed and bound by
Gutenberg Press Ltd
MALTA

CONTENTS

In memory of
my beloved wife

Maureen

Acknowledgements

I would like to record my appreciation of the assistance provided by the staff of the archives section of the University of Bangor Library; Gwynedd Archive Service; Anglesey Record Office; Bangor Museum; Welsh Slate Museum; Caernarfon Library; Royal College of Physicians and Surgeons, Glasgow; Rev. Lloyd Jones, St Mary's Church, Felinheli; Dr Peter Ellis Jones; Dr Katie Lench and David Longley.

There are many others who provided assistance in various ways including: Rita Bishop; Ken Brown; Glyn Foulkes; Robert and Maureen Howes; Arnold Hughes; Cadi Iolen; Alun L. Jones; Helen Jones; Eric Lander; Keith Morris, Joe Heber Owen; Michael and Ann Roberts; Stanley and Kathleen W. Roberts; T. Arfon Roberts; W. Wyn and Helen Roberts; Joan Rowe; Colin Ryan; Peter Thompson; Ieuan Wyn Williams; Sylvia Williams and W. Robin Williams.

My thanks also to Bethan Smith for allowing me access to her collection of material and photographs relating to her family and the village, also to Len V. Williams for readily providing copies of photographs from his collection. In particular, my thanks to W. Alister Williams for his advice and guidance.

Abbreviations & Placenames

AC	Author's collection		MN	Merchant Navy
BP	Bangor Papers		NWC	*North Wales Chronicle*
C&DH	*Caernarvon & Denbigh Herald*		NWG	*North Wales Guardian*
CQS	Caernarfon Quarter Sessions		RN	Royal Navy
CWGC	Commonwealth War Graves		RNR	Royal Naval Reserve
	Commission		UWB	University of Wales, Bangor
DQ	Dinorwic Quarry		VP	Vaynol Papers
GAS	Gwynedd Archives Service			

The changes in the spelling of place names causes some confusion. Throughout the text, the modern spelling of Caernarfon has been used, but the archaic anglicised spellings of Carnarvon and Caernarvon have been retained in specific place names e.g. Caernarvon Turnpike Trust, or in direct quotations. The archaic spelling of Vaynol has been used throughout the text as that was the spelling in common use during the period covered by this book. Likewise, the name Port Dinorwic has been used rather than the original and present day name Y Felinheli.

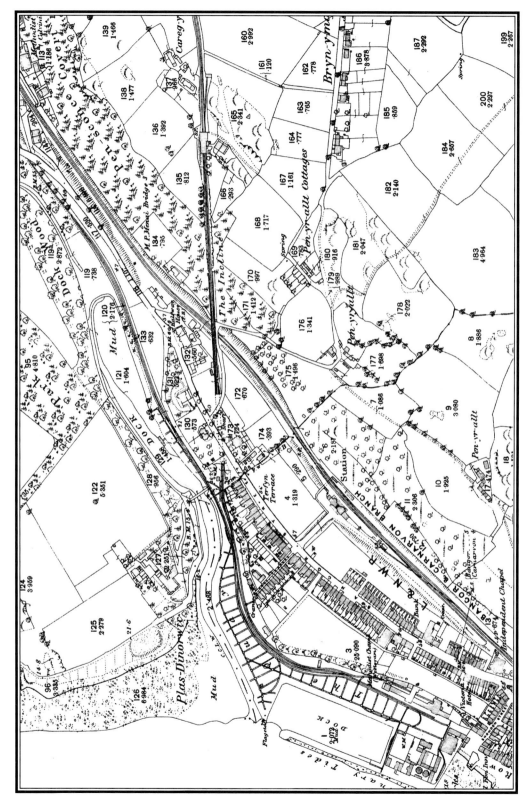

1889 OS map of the northern section of Port Dinorwic showing the original docks, the incline from Penscoins, the L&NWR line and the developed area of the village between the junction of Snowdon Street/Bangor Street and the Halfway House Inn.

INTRODUCTION

The present day settlement of Y Felinheli, sited roughly halfway between the old county town of Caernarfon and the city of Bangor can be passed unnoticed by travellers speeding along the modern by-pass which was opened in 1994. Until then, all traffic had to wend its way through the main street of what was a ribbon development sited on the eastern shore of the Menai Strait and which, for less than a century, was known by the name of Port Dinorwic.

The history of this village is a microcosm of the history of central Caernarfonshire during the past two hundred years, developing as it did from a couple of small hamlets into a significant port for the export of slate to far-flung corners of the world. The population grew from a few dozen mainly agricultural workers into several thousands who worked in the slate industry, centred upon the great Dinorwic Quarry at Llanberis, or in the shipping industry which serviced it. As the numbers employed in these primary industries grew, particularly during the period 1850–1914, so they attracted a variety of other workers – retailers, innkeepers, doctors, teachers, ministers of religion, etc – who provided the essential services required by any community at that time.

With the decline of the slate industry during the first half of the twentieth century, so the village was obliged to reinvent itself and today it is mainly a dormitory settlement for people who work in Bangor or Caernarfon, or who sail the Strait for pleasure. At one time, Port Dinorwic supported well over fifty retail premises. Today there is just one shop, with customers driving the few miles to the large supermarkets in the neighbouring towns.

This monograph attempts to piece together the story of the growth of Y Felinheli and the changes that it has witnessed over the last 200 years, just as it comes to terms with its new role at the start of the twenty-first century.

Any history of Y Felinheli or Port Dinorwic must weave its story with threads drawn from the nearby Faenol (Vaynol) estate which played such an essential part in its development. Likewise the history cannot be told without significant reference to the Dinorwic Quarry as without one the other would not have risen to such prominence. This is not, however, a history of the Faenol estate or the Dinorwic Quarry, that has already been told in my previous publications, most notably *Dinorwic – the Llanberis Slate Quarry*, and *Sailing the Strait*. I did publish an earlier work entitled *Felinheli – a personal history of the port of Dinorwic*; this book attempts to expand upon that work and to draw into the story the new material that has come to light during the last quarter of a century.

The coastal area today known as Y Felinheli in the parish of Llanfairisgaer, grew around two hamlets, Aberpwll and Tafarngrisiau, sited just over a mile apart along the main Bangor to Caernarfon highway. When the original water mill at Aberpwll, under the control of the bishop of Bangor, became inoperative due to the irregularity of the Afon Heilyn, a small river that flowed

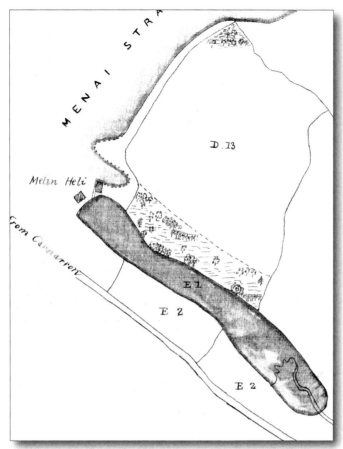

down Nant-y-Garth, a new mill was constructed on the side of the mud inlet in a position where it would derive the maximum benefit from the tidal flow of the Menai Strait. Initially the new site appears to have been called Aber Heilyn and, eventually Felinheli (salt water mill).

Thomas Assheton Smith's agent, Thomas Wright, refers in his 1793 accounts to 'Cottage at salt mill' tenanted by the Dinorwic Slate Company. [GAS VP4322] Five years later, the same tenant holds what is described as the 'old mill bank and quay'. [GAS VP4057]

According to a report in *Yr Herald Gymraeg* of 8 October 1864 the name of the last miller was given as William Gray and that it was by *c*.1797 'greatly out of repair'. By *c*.1810, the few wharfs that had been built within the estuary at least allowed an alternative

Site of the Melin Heli. E 1 is described as 'Mill Kiln Bank & Pool'   method of loading small schooners
[GAS]   of about 100 tons with slate rather that the time-consuming method of

lightering (transferring goods to and from ships by means of large open boats). [UWB X/AA7CAR]

Prior to the building of the new dock at Port Dinorwic at the end of the nineteenth century, there had been discussion as to the location of the old salt water mill which gave its name to Felinheli. Ernest Neale, agent to the Vaynol estate, in his letter [Hasties, London 2.11.1903] shows:

Before employing anyone to discover the site of the old mill it occurred to me that it would be a wise thing to have the quarry engineer down from Llanberis and see what he would make of the question. I gave him the old estate plans and instructed him to prove from these the site of the old mill and he located the site of the old mill close to the inner gate of the lock. On comparing this with Oswell's (the engineer who built the new dock) plan it coincides with where that gentleman records having found the old foundations of the mill and also with where the mill is shewn by Mr Fred Jackson's other Vaynol Estate plans. In face of these facts Mr Vivian and myself think that it is hardly necessary to employ any other surveyor unless you and Mr

Danctwort are still of opinion that it would be advisable. [GAS DQ2765, 6, 7, 2777, 2778, VP2379, XD88/4/331]

Although the plans referred to have not been found, other archival material confirms the mill's position at the head of the pool of retained water which, when released at the time of slack water, enabled the mill to continue working. As a result of the changes made during the rebuilding of the harbour, the mill would have been positioned on the Caernarfon side of the harbour near to the inside lock, but obviously at a lower level (see Chapter 3 and illustrations).

The Halfway House, sited as the name suggests roughly equidistant between Caernarfon and Bangor, figured prominently in the life of the village until mid-nineteenth century. It had a licence to brew its own beer in 1860 but the licence issued to Margaret Jones limited the quantity to twenty barrels per annum. The beer which was kept cool in the cellar, was served at the bar from jugs. When the harbour was being built, the navvies did not have far to walk for their supply of beer since the tavern was open all day until 11 p.m. In addition to catering for the traveller, an extension was added in 1836 to accommodate a shop. Five years later, a post office was established at the tavern followed by a new coach house built in 1843. [GAS VP4477, XQA/L/9/191] The 1967 sale catalogue, which suggests that the inn was established some 300 years ago,

Lewis Morris's map of the Menai Strait showing the Mill, the Holly Bush, the Gardd Fôn and Dinas.

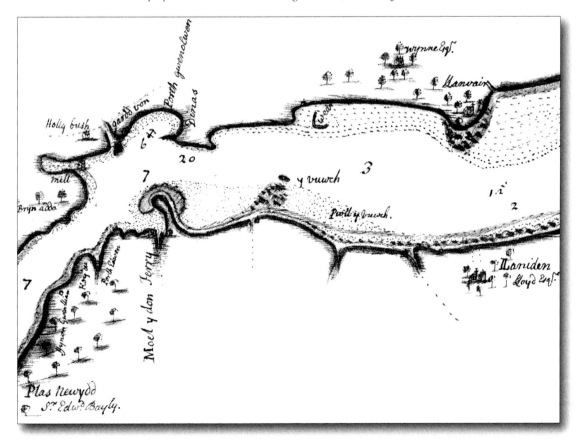

described the property as including a stone and slate pigsty and pound stable, tack room, coach-house, two loose boxes, small garden with lawn, vegetable garden and greenhouse. Other than the tavern, the only other properties between the two hamlets of Aberpwll and Tafarngrisiau were Terfyn cottage and Bush Farm.

As a result of the 1812 road being built from the quarry to the quay to facilitate the transport of slate, the long-established hamlet of Aberpwll extended to the area known as Siloh where cottages were provided for the additional workforce. Even though it was only a small community, three chapels had been built there by 1861 and the children had the benefit of a small private school which provided a basic education at a cost to the parents of one penny a week, at a time when education was usually limited to that of the Sunday school.

There were few changes until 1848 when the Padarn line, running between the Dinorwic Quarry and Penscoins, was completed, and four years later, the arrival of the Bangor to Caernarfon main line railway. The two events proved to be the catalyst for further significant developments including the establishment of a new village between the two hamlets mentioned.

Compared to the long established Welsh-named farms of Bodandreg (CQS 20 May 1552), Carreg Gwalch, Pant-yr-Afallen and Penrallt, Bush farm appears to be incongruously named. It may well have been adapted from the original name of Holly Bush (as shown on the previously mentioned Lewis Morris's 1748 map) confirmed by 1737 records which describe it as being a tavern where drovers had secure compounds for their animals where they could rest overnight and have access to water and feed (drovers generally were aware of such facilities provided by similarly named taverns in various parts of the country). Legal documents were still referring to it as Bush Tavern in 1861. [UWB MSS 1162]

From 1820 when Thomas Assheton Smith took control of the Dinorwic Quarry, the quantity of slate being produced increased significantly. As the quantity of slate arriving on the quayside increased, correspondingly so did the number of men employed. However, even though it had become apparent that land would be required for properties to be built, this could only be accomplished on Bush farmland which, together with the greater part of the parish of Llanfairisgaer, belonged to Lord Boston. Consequently, any expansion of the quayside for additional slate storage by Assheton Smith required Boston's authority (see Shops, Trades and Houses chapter for subsequent developments).

1: VAYNOL

In the sixteenth century, when the bishops of Bangor began to sell property belonging to their manor, Maenol (Vaynol) Bangor, the Williams family of Cochwillan acquired land that eventually encompassed most of the parishes of Llanddeiniolen and Llanberis as far as, and including, Snowdon. This is where Thomas Wyn ap William (d.1592), also known as Thomas Williams, a member of the established gentry family of Cochwillan, took up residence in the late sixteenth century. The dowry that resulted from his marriage (c.1570) to Jane, the eldest daughter of the powerful Stanley family, earls of Derby, with estates in Hooton, Cheshire, west Lancashire and Caernarfonshire, may well have been beneficial at the time when he built the Tudor house (now known as Faenol Old Hall) that became the focal point of Faenol. Thomas Williams's policy of expansion and consolidation of land in the area resulted in the Vaynol estate owning over 23,000 acres by the 1660s.

The mansion was unusual in north Wales in having a chapel built within the grounds between 1560 and 1580. It was dedicated to St Mary and a carved stone within the porch bears the initials 'WW' and 'E' William Williams (the son of Thomas Williams) and Ellen – his first wife. The other contemporary building of note a short distance away from the mansion is the large barn built in

Vaynol Old Hall [GAS]

13

1605, which bears the initials 'WW' and 'D' (William Williams and Dorothy – his second wife). By the 1630s, Vaynol Hall had been extended to almost four times the size of the original house.

When Sir William Williams (the sixth baronet) died without heirs in 1696, the estate was left to three members of the Wrey family of Tawstock, Devon during their lifetime. Thereafter, it reverted to the Crown before being gifted by King William III to a Hampshire family called Smith in 1699. [GAS VP3560]

Thomas Assheton Smith (1752–1828)

Thomas Assheton Smith (1776–1858)

Thomas Assheton Smith (1752–1828)

Thomas Assheton Smith inherited the estate in 1774. He married Elizabeth, the daughter of Watkin Wynn of Foelas, and they had three sons and five daughters. In 1783–4, he served as High Sheriff of Carnarvonshire and he was Member of Parliament for the county from 1774–80. In 1809, he was appointed a lieutenant-colonel in the Carnarvonshire Regiment of Local Militia. [GAS Pool 30]

Shortly after 1780, Assheton Smith decided to build a new gentleman's villa and stables designed by Bangor architect, James Defferd, for a fee of £600. Work on the new property, Vaynol House as it became known, was started in 1793 and an interim payment of £100 to Defferd is shown in the 1794 accounts. [GAS VP4322]

The new house was situated a short distance from Faenol Old Hall and was an obvious status symbol. The property was a declaration of intent, an indication of his significant interest in the estate and local matters. By 1785, Faenol Old Hall was being used by Thomas Wright, Assheton Smith's agent. On Assheton Smith's death in 1828, he was succeeded by his second son who bore the same name as himself (his first son having died in childhood). [GAS DQ1, VP4322]

Thomas Assheton Smith (1776–1858)

During the 1840s when Thomas Assheton Smith II set about consolidating his estate by selling outlying lands including those in Cheshire, the Conwy valley and Llŷn, [GAS VP4193–4196] the monies realised were reinvested in local projects, such as the purchase of Fachwen Farm from Lord Newborough, and land was exchanged with the Glynllifon and Penrhyn estates. In 1850, possibly as part of this pro-

Top: Vaynol House. The single-storey wing on the far left has since been demolished. [AC]
Above left: Vaynol, sitting room.
Above right: Vaynol, the staircase.
Bottom left: The study at Vaynol.

gramme of consolidation, he purchased the Bryn Tirion property that adjoined his estate. [GAS XM/543/18]

Having failed to purchase Plas Newydd from the Marquis of Anglesey, Assheton Smith set about extending Vaynol House to approximately three times its original size. Such was the extent of the rebuilding work that he and his wife were obliged to rent Plas Newydd from the Marquis of Anglesey.

George William Duff Assheton Smith (1848–1904)

When Thomas Assheton Smith died at Vaynol he was buried at the family seat of Tedworth in Hampshire. As he had no children, his estate went to George William Duff, the grandson of his sister, Elizabeth Assheton Smith by her marriage to William Buckler Astley. Until George William Duff inherited the estate on his twenty-first birthday in 1869 and assumed the names Assheton Smith, its administration was the responsibility of his father, Captain Robert George Duff, as trustee, who continued with Assheton Smith's policy of disposing of distant lands and investing the proceeds locally. A survey undertaken in 1869 indicated that the estate's total acreage had increased to 38,158 acres.

When Captain Duff decided to build a wall around the home park at Vaynol, the section of the Bangor to Caernarfon toll road that ran through the grounds had to be redirected to follow the contour of the eventual wall. In addition, the old toll house (which may well have been the property now known as Hen Efail since no other building is shown on contemporary maps) was replaced by one at Capel Graig in 1863. [GAS VP6896] Also built at this time was a cottage named Gwerngogas near to the present Grand Lodge at a cost of £151 'for forester'.

The initial work on the wall in 1863 entailed the 'clearing of ground and labourers and others walling and fencing out New Plantation and clearing old fences at a cost of £186 13s 8d'. [UWB Edern papers 38] As a result, a number of cottages, including Tyddyn Maelog near the old Aberpwll mill, were demolished in anticipation of the wall being built, and the people affected

were rehoused in the newly-built Singrig and Penrallt cottages. The stone for the wall was extracted from various quarries on the estate and the lime from the kiln by Afon Odyn near Brynadda.

Labourers' wages during March 1864 relating to the diverting of the turnpike road near Vaenol lodge came to £55 2s 0d while 'mettling' of the new road cost £4 11s 3d. Owing to the large quantity of stone brought from the quarry at Brynadda and the damage caused to the roadway, an entry appears in the agent's account book for 'labourers repairing road to Brynadda Building Stone Quarry cut by cartage of stone for Park Wall £5 4s 0d'.

Captain Duff was in regular contact with his agent, Millington, whenever he was away from the estate. In a letter dated 23

George William Duff Assheton Smith (1848–1904). [GAS]

Vaynol Hall library.

Vaynol the Princess of Wales's bedroom.

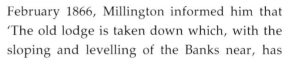

February 1866, Millington informed him that 'The old lodge is taken down which, with the sloping and levelling of the Banks near, has already improved the appearance of the new approach entrance [it] shows itself perfectly now that the Wall across the old road is partly up'. The 1866 records reveal that 'one third of the distance up Vaynol hill from Tŷ Golchi had been built and 'a short gap [had been left] where the intended Grand Lodge [was] to be located. The whole of the wall along the Menai Strait shore is still to be built'. [GAS VP4126]

The new main entrance, or the Grand Lodge as it was called, incorporated a bay on each side of the old road to allow horse-drawn carriages to negotiate a circle. Apart from the Grand Lodge, four additional lodges or entrances were incorporated into the wall, together with a door close to Treborth station for the benefit of those who lived nearby. Perhaps the most colourful of lodge keepers was Charles Mackenzie who started work at Bryntirion lodge in 1893. Having been the a pipe major in the 2nd Battalion, King's Own Scottish Borderers, he was regularly seen marching up and down the drive leading to the lodge in his clan uniform playing the bagpipes.

By 1869, when George W.D. Assheton Smith took charge of the estate and had made Vaynol his home, pointing work to the wall had been completed. The final touches of masons making caps for the lodges and principal entrance was completed in 1870 and by the following year, the carving of the arms had been executed and the gates painted. The total cost of the wall was £25,098 16s 2d. Before the wall was completed, the Assheton Smiths had been little more than a name to most people in Caernarfonshire; the new wall merely increased their isolation.

Not only did the Vaynol wall guarantee privacy for the family, it also provided a secure environment for the variety of animals introduced by Assheton Smith in 1872. These included white Chillingham cattle whose temperament was completely unpredictable as far as humans were concerned, together with zebras and two or more varieties of deer. In the tradition of Victorian trophy collecting and wild animal display, Assheton Smith had dangerous animals such

The Grand Lodge (the gates were made by D.J. Williams of Caernarfon). [GAS]

Bryntirion Lodge.

as bears in secure enclosures within a menagerie which was built in January 1870. [GAS VP2399, 7323]

In his quest for additional 'unusual or exotic animals', changes in the menagerie took place from time to time with animals being bought, sold or even exchanged as indicated in a letter sent by William Lort, Assheton Smith's secretary and manager at Vaynol, to Charles Harris on 18 May 1900 which read:

> I agree to give the stork and the cormorant and ten pounds for the two bear cubs which I conclude are less than half-grown otherwise they would be of no use here … a steamer will call for the cubs in about a fortnight's time, please put them in a crate.

A later letter referred to the stork and the cormorant and informed the recipient that 'they had been fed on fish and should have it to thrive. I believe they are sometimes fed on fresh Sheep's tripe and the stork will eat frogs'!

An offer of £30 was made by Mr Assheton Smith for a pair of Wapiti deer on condition that 'they were thoroughly healthy and absolutely pure bred.' [GAS VP2379]

If a surplus of animals occurred, then an advertisement was placed in *The Bazaar* magazine. The insertion for August 1900 stated that the following animals were for sale but prices were not stated for all the items: 'Pumas £46 pair, Tiger cat £3, Genet £2 10s 0d, Black ape female, Capuchin male, Hybrid silver pheasant, Golden Eagle £4, 2 Jackals £6, 2 adult Emus £20, Rhea £6, White Goats, four horned Black Sheep …' Deer were sold periodically and in 1901, there was correspondence with D.F. Carlin of Leslie, South Dakota, USA regarding the possible purchase of a herd of forty-five American bison at a price of $500 each.

It was reported in a local newspaper that Mr Assheton Smith had lost 'a fine specimen of a

Griffon Vulture, a native of Southern Europe and Africa.' Its body was presented to the University College Bangor. The report also stated that 'he presented to the college a magnificent Wapiti stag some time ago'. (NWC 7 December 1901)

The *Exchange & Mart* for 1901 advertised white wolves at £20 while in 1902 the Vaynol menagerie was selling '2 Malay Bears (very tame), 3 part bred Ibex, 1 Bonnet Monkey, 2 Mandrills, 2 Marmots, 2 Lemurs etc'. Further additions included leopards, pumas and boars. Although Lort had inserted an advertisement in the magazine, 'Wanted energetic young man unmarried to look after Birds, Monkeys and other animals in a private Menagerie. Must have done similar work before.' By 1905, the decision had been taken to dispose of the zoological collection. [GAS VP4427, 4428, 4498]

As a means of controlling the abundance of rabbits, hares and birds on the estate shooting parties were arranged from time to time. Although numbers varied from year to year as to the number shot, some idea can be gleaned from the figures recorded on 1 March 1895: 'Grouse 124, Hares 457, Pheasants 334, Partridge 117, Snipe 75, Wild fowl 182, Woodcock 65, Rabbit 8,050.' When the number shot was in excess of that needed for 'home' consumption, the opportunity was taken to distribute game to those who had served the estate in one capacity or another. The 'Game Given Away' book dated 1905–6 gives detail of the recipients ranging from local dignitaries such as doctors, ministers, station master, school masters, bank manager and shopkeepers to the many employees of the estate.

Sir Charles Garden Duff Assheton Smith, Bt (1815–1914)
When George Assheton Smith died in 1904, he became the first of the family to be interred in Vaynol. The estate then passed to Charles Garden Duff Assheton Smith who married Sybil, the sister of W.W. Vivian from The Glyn, Bangor. Created a baronet in 1911, he proved to be a lavish

Banners at Port Dinorwic welcome the Duke and Duchess of York 1899. [GAS]

Charles G.D. Assheton Smith with a Grand National winner. [GAS]

spender, especially as far as the pleasures of life were concerned. A successful racehorse owner, he had three winners in the Grand National: 1893 *Cloister*; 1912 *Jerry M* and 1913 *Covertcoat* as well as a number of well-placed horses. Such was his interest in horses that the stables at Vaynol were fitted out opulently by Young and Company in 1913.

A list of the employees at Vaynol Hall in 1904, together with their annual salary, gives an indication of the various positions within the household: G. Bagg, house steward – £100; M.G. Moss, Valet – £55; W. Crow, footman – £36; Albert Stork, footman – £30; John Holmes, hall porter – £39; Mrs Harris, cook – £65; Mrs Hopson, maid – £50; Miss Grant, maid – £35; Mina Smith, 1st housemaid – £30; M. Downs, 2nd housemaid – £22; H. Gibson, 3rd housemaid – £18; E. Parker, 4th housemaid – £16; A. Jarvis, kitchen maid – £26; A. Norris, 2nd kitchen maid – £22; L. Orbell, scullery maid – £16. The head gardener was H. Weaver and his assistant was G. Griffin (who was later to become head gardener). They led a team who were responsible for the gardens and in particular, the regular supply of fruit and vegetables for the mansion.

Vaynol House had the capacity to accommodate not only the family and guests but also many of the staff. At the time of Sir Charles Assheton Smith, all the staff would have their appropriate uniform including the seven dairymaids who were dressed in blue with black stockings.

Those employees working and living within sight of the mansion who had children, ensured that they did not stray anywhere near the building or the main drive, although in retrospect, the consensus of opinion was that there would not have been any repercussions had any children been seen near to the purported forbidden territory.

At the beginning of the twentieth century, the first sign of modernisation appeared in Vaynol in the form of an electric generator which was installed to produce sufficient

Vaynol estate workers, January 1911. The farm bailiff on the left is George Roddick. [Vera Roberts]

power for the mansion and ancillary buildings on the estate. With a view to possibly improving communication, a letter to the National Telephone Company in March 1905 read 'Mr Assheton Smith accepts the offer of the National Telephone Company to give a direct telephone service between Vaynol and Bangor … [he] does not accept the Company's offer for a service to the Estate Office'. Indeed the estate office had to wait until after the First World War to be connected to the telephone system.

Vaynol estate workers. [T. Arfon Roberts]

Sir Charles died on 14 September 1914 and was buried in Vaynol church.

Sir Michael Robert Vivian Duff Assheton Smith (1907–80)

Robert (Robin) George Vivian Duff, who succeeded to the title and estate in 1914, was killed in France at the start of the First World War and the estate was held in trust for his seven year old son and successor, Michael Robert Vivian Duff Assheton Smith.

Sir Michael, who dropped the use of the names Assheton Smith in 1945, had many friends in the world of the arts and the theatre and it was not unknown for a guest to arrive by aeroplane, landing in the main park. One such person was a Mr Tong and if he decided to fly at night, as he was inclined to, then as many cars as possible would be assembled with their headlights switched on to indicate the landing path.

Some of the guests staying at Vaynol would travel by road and others by rail or, in the case of the Duke of Sutherland, who was a regular summer visitor, would arrive in a yacht which would be moored on the Strait. Evening parties alternated between the hall and the yacht where bagpipes could be heard playing both plaintive and lively music. Queen Elizabeth, the Queen Mother, was a frequent visitor to Vaynol as indeed was Princess Marina, Duchess of Kent. The commanding 6ft 4ins figure of Sir Michael was to be seen as often at local functions as it was with the Royal family in London.

When Sir Michael returned to Vaynol after a period in the forces during the Second World War (he had served as a flying officer in the Royal Air Force intelligence unit), he had some difficulty in getting the previously smooth programme of life on the estate back into operation. This may have been caused by a change in attitude towards the 'squire' after the experiences many employees had encountered during the war. An attempt made to restart the estate laundry at Brynadda in 1944 met with difficulties due to 'the person responsible procrastinating to the annoyance of Sir Michael' according to the agent. The laundryman's salary was £400 per annum from which he was expected to pay for any extra labour required, purchase soaps, cleaning materials, coal which was purchased from the estate, and electricity. War-time conditions still prevailed and many of the items were still rationed and could only be purchased with the use of coupons.

Sir Michael Duff Assheton Smith. [GAS]

Farmer tenants had to conform with the conditions imposed by the estate and if it was noted that insufficient care was being taken of farm land, resulting in an abundance of weed, then a strong letter would be sent to the farmer concerned instructing him to bring the land back to its proper condition.

The autocratic attitude of the Vaynol agent towards the employees for bad workmanship or behaviour could result in instant dismissal with no right of appeal. Such a dogmatic attitude had been accepted before the Second World War, but those who returned from the conflict had very different experiences in the forces and did not feel obliged to return to their old lifestyle in the village or to their former occupation, if better opportunities presented themselves elsewhere.

In what was considered a philanthropic gesture, workers were retired from time to time, although many continued working, health permitting, until they were in their seventies. This presumably was the reason for sending a letter to Mr R. Davies, Brynadda on 24 April 1945 stating that in view of his long illness, Sir Michael considered it best for him to retire and that he proposed giving him a pension of 12s 6d per week, plus an allowance of £15 per annum, to enable him to pay rent for a house which he would have to find himself. Sir Michael wished him 'every happiness in his retirement' after the long period that he had served the estate.

Following Sir Michael's marriage in 1935 to Lord Tweedmouth's daughter, the Hon. Joan Marjoribanks (which only lasted two years), he married Lady Caroline Paget, sister of the Marquis of Anglesey in 1949. There were no children from either marriage, but they adopted a boy named Charles David Duff.

When the investiture of the Prince of Wales took place in 1969 at Caernarfon Castle, members of the Royal family stayed at Vaynol and it was thought that never before had so many of them been assembled under one roof, except for Buckingham Palace.

Lady Caroline died in 1976 and Sir Michael on 3 March 1980, aged 72, and the Vaynol estate, which had existed for about 450 years, came to an end. With the demise of the estate and the consequential loss of employment, the character of the delightful, if not unique, village of Felinheli changed completely and irrevocably.

2: Dinorwic Quarry

Some 33,000 acres of the Snowdonia range, including Snowdon itself, were owned by the Vaynol estate which, towards the end of the eighteenth century, was the second largest in Caernarfonshire.

When the second Thomas Assheton Smith (1776–1858) inherited the estate in 1828, it was at a time when there was an increasing demand for a durable and reliable roofing material for factories and houses. Slate had all the necessary characteristics for roofing, irrespective of the weather or the adverse atmospheric conditions that were prevalent during the Industrial Revolution. Being free of fossils, and available in a variety of colours, slate can be split longitudinally, each split being as good as the original stone. The slate found in the north-west corner of Wales is the hardest in the world and is far superior to that produced in any other country.

Slate had been quarried on a casual basis by individuals for their own benefit until 1787 when Assheton Smith granted a lease of twenty-one years to three individuals who traded as the Dinorwic Slate Company. When the lease expired, Assheton Smith offered William Turner (father of Sir Llewelyn Turner of Parkia, Caernarfon) a partnership in the Llanberis quarry on condition that he came to live in the neighbourhood. What Turner found was a quarry being worked in a very primitive manner. One innovation that he introduced when he took over was the notion of inclined planes which allowed easier transport of slate down the mountain side. The partnership continued until 1820 when Assheton Smith took full control by buying Turner's share, no doubt realising the future potential of slate. The Dinorwic quarry, covering around 800 acres, was the largest in the world.

From the 1820s, men who had previously been employed in agriculture or cottage industries began to be drawn to the quarry or its ancillary services such as transport. Sufficient men were available in nearby villages for the methods then being used and the quantity of slate produced but, with an increasing demand for roofing slate and changes in the method of transport, came a need to recruit more workers.

Slate is a wasteful product since approximately 85% of the original stone is discarded during the production process which resulted in a vast amount of slate waste accumulating on the mountain side of Elidir leaving it heavily scarred. Even now, over a hundred years since production was at its height, there is little vegetation growing amongst it. The vast terraces descending down the side of the mountain give some indication of the hardship that men and boys endured, irrespective of weather conditions.

The transportation of slate from quarry to coast during the second half of the eighteenth

The Nant-y-Garth road, built in 1812, was the route taken by the tramway in 1824. [Bethan Smith]

century was done by means of panniers on the back of mules or horses but, by the turn of the century, improvements to the roads allowed horses and carts to be used which were hired from local farmers. Apart from being a costly exercise, the lack of continuity in the provision of transport inevitably affected the quantity of slate that could be transported to the coast even when the demand for roofing slate increased. Assheton Smith decided in 1812 to build a new private road connecting Llanddeiniolen with Aberpwll inlet where improvements to the wharf continued to be made. Twelve years later, rather than be dependent upon the farming fraternity providing costly transport, a seven mile railroad (*ffordd haearn*) was built at a total cost of £9,000.

The wagons, with double-flanged wheels, began their journey on the 1ft 10ins gauge railroad, at the quarries above Llyn Peris before descending through two inclines, then heading towards Clwt-y-Bont. From there, the railroad followed more or less the 1812 road until it reached the third incline above Nant-y-Garth. For the last mile or so before it reached the Aberpwll inlet, it passed through a tunnel built of stone beneath the Bangor to Caernarfon turnpike road (a feature which may have been at the insistence of the Caernarvonshire Turnpike Trust). The last half-mile ran alongside Afon Heilyn until it reached the improved wharfs where the slate was loaded onto small schooners or lightered to ships anchored on the strait. From its highest point at Allt Ddu to sea level it had dropped about 1,000 feet giving it a gradient, excluding the three inclines, of 1:40.

The railroad began operating in March 1825 and the quantity of slate transported between quarry and port increased to 16,046 tons between January and September 1829, at a cost of eight shillings per ton. [GAS DQ1974] It appears that the quantity of slate to be conveyed to the port was under-estimated since a further sixty wagons were ordered in April 1825, 'in addition to 200, contracted for' at a cost of £420.

By the mid 1830s, Assheton Smith realised that the method of transporting slate produced at lower levels up the hill to Allt Ddu was uneconomical, especially at a time of increasing demand, and decided that a new railway system had to be introduced with a much higher carrying capacity. Although he owned a great deal of the land between his estate at Vaynol and the parish of Llanddeiniolen where the slate was being produced, he was restricted in any possible future

Two views of the 1824 tunnel constructed near Bryntirion Lodge to enable horse-drawn wagons to pass beneath the tollroad. Left: the entrance before it was sealed. Right: the interior of the tunnel. [AC]

developments since land adjoining his own, including Fachwen farm which extended from Allt Ddu to the shore of Llyn Padarn, was owned by Lord Newborough. It was imperative that he must acquire this land if his intention of building a new railway was to materialise. Lord Newborough realised from the start how important it was to Assheton Smith that he acquire the land and pitched the selling price accordingly. If the planned purchase failed, then the construction of a new railway system alongside the lake would be difficult, if not impossible. Newborough agreed to a ninety-nine year lease on the 234 acres of land for £15,000, but retained mineral right on Fachwen. [GAS XD2 19033] Assheton Smith writing to his agent, Owen Roberts, on 9 February 1840, stated that he would not even contemplate paying royalties and believed that the price was too high 'for the rocky small farm which he cannot let in parts to quarrymen'. Eventually, after some acrimonious correspondence, it was agreed that Newborough would sell the freehold for £13,500 (present day approximate value £600,000). [GAS XD2 1906]

The purchase, which was completed on 30 June 1840, enabled the Padarn Railway to be built. It also allowed slate waste, an ever increasing problem, to be dumped on the hillside above Llyn Padarn and the lake itself, so allowing land adjacent to Glan-y-Bala to be reclaimed. The problem of transporting slate from quarries adjacent to Llyn Peris to Gilfach Ddu was solved by building a connecting tunnel through the Glan-y-Bala rock. The reclamation of land not only allowed the Padarn Railway terminus to be built, it also provided, after a great deal more waste had been dumped, a base for the Gilfach Ddu complex that was built in 1870.

The construction of the railway line from Gilfach Ddu to Port Dinorwic, a distance of six miles five furlongs, was undertaken by 135 groups of men, each working a 'bargain' with an agreed contract price for a specific task within an allocated section. The greatest cost in the construction was the building of bridges and also the use of explosives to remove rocks for a cutting on the northern shores of Llyn Padarn. Waste slate blocks were used to build a retaining wall as a means of strengthening the bed of the eventual railway track along the shore of the lake.

From May 1841 a new heading 'The New Railroad called Padarn Railway' appeared in the quarry accounts. Iron rails were imported from Newport, south Wales in November 1841 and delivered to Port Dinorwic aboard the schooner *William* before being transported to Glan-y-Bala. Even though the railway started operating in March 1843, the 1824 Fachwen to Port Dinorwic railroad ran contemporaneously with it for a short while, possibly as a convenient way of clearing the stock of slates in the Allt Ddu area. In July 1843, 4,134 tons of slates were transported on the new railroad confirming its completion as far as the horse-hauling operation was concerned.

By June 1842, as part of the Padarn line building programme, houses and a shop were built at Carreg-y-Walch, near Penscoins, to accommodate the railway workers. Also, stables were provided along the line (such as *Stablau* near Llanrug) for use of the horses that hauled the trucks during the period of construction and during its first five years of operation.

Whilst construction was taking place, hundreds of stone blocks were prepared at a cost of 1s 3d each for use as sleepers (the use of blocks allowed horses an easier passage whilst hauling trucks). Treenails (defined as long wooden pins or nails used to fasten the planks of a ship to the timbers) for fastening the rail chairs were also being made out of oak-wood at a cost of £5 per thousand. Although there is no mention of the size of gauge in use, it can be assumed that it was 4ft from the outset.

In addition to constructing the railway from Gilfach Ddu to Port Dinorwic, a 1,250ft long incline, with a 1 in 4½ mean gradient, had to be built from Penscoins, to the quayside. Part of the incline passed through a tunnel, measuring 10ft x 8ft, beneath the Caernarfon to Bangor road. In addition to a place of safety within it, a hut was provided halfway down the incline for the benefit

The Dinorwic Slate Quarry which dominated the landscape alongside Llyn Padarn.

The Penscoins incline c.1896 operating with chains before it was replaced by wire ropes [GAS]

of the person responsible for the general maintenance of the incline, including oiling the iron rollers between the rails upon which the chain ran. Wagons were attached to the continuous chain in groups of four, but such a cumbersome method required the chain to be stopped frequently to attach full wagons at the top of the incline and empty ones at the bottom (this was replaced in later years with a wire rope). As a safety measure, each wagon was chained together. An open-ended shed was constructed in September 1845 at Penscoins to give protection from the weather for both the equipment used at the top of the incline and also the men responsible for the incline operation. The total cost of constructing the Padarn railway and incline and the provision of stables, was £35,952 12s 6½d. [GAS XD40/2/32]

In order that the railway could be used to transport men to and from the quarry, velocipedes or *ceir gwyllt*, as they were called, were introduced in 1848. The fifty-two vehicles sporting such names as *Nelson, Wylfa, Fox, Grant, Garibaldi, Blondin, Bught, Jimbol, Jennie Bach, Black Bess, Livingstone, Stag* and *Express*, were bought by groups of quarrymen. Each vehicle was registered in the Gilfach Ddu quarry office with the signature or mark of the man responsible for it. Permission had to be obtained before they could be used on the railway and, when given, instructions were issued that '[passengers] shall not get on or off while in motion [they were] not to travel at a speed to endanger the persons riding in them or any other person'. *Ceir gwyllt* (examples of which may be seen at both the Welsh Slate Museum in Llanberis and at Penrhyn Castle Railway Museum in Bangor) carried up to sixteen men depending on the size and design and provided no protection from the weather. They were as dangerous to passengers as they were to anyone they encountered on the journey and on 15 September 1892, Isaac Parry and Hugh Griffith wrote to the quarry agent on behalf of all velocipede riders, asking for a better mode of conveyance to and from the quarry stating that 'the existing velocipedes [was] both dangerous to limb and laborious to propel'.

In July 1848, a payment of £733 was made to Alfred Horlock & Company of Northfleet, Kent

Left, a multi-seater velocipede that conveyed quarrymen to work along the Padarn line c.1869 and, right, a cycle-type velocipede. [AC]

for a 'locomotive engine for the railway'. Within five years of the line being opened, two steam locomotives, *Jenny Lind* and *Fire Queen*, along with their tenders, had been purchased at a total cost of £2,397. Both were of a 0-4-0 tender engine design, with wheels 4ft 6ins in diameter and a wheel-base of 12ft 0½ins. Instead of conventional frames, the locomotives were, like a traction engine, built around the 8ft 3½ins long boiler barrel. The two outside 13ins x 22ins inclined cylinders, mounted on the elevated boiler, transmitted power to the rear wheels. The boiler, fed by coke (both engines were later adapted to burn coal) from the tender with its 3ft 6ins diameter wheels, produced steam at 60lb/sq. in. Its conspicuous five-foot high chimney had a 13ins diameter. Both engines originally operated without the benefit of a cab but *Jenny Lind* had one fitted later and, having had new tubes and bearings in 1877, continued in service until 1882 when she was scrapped. Fortunately, when *Fire Queen* was taken out of service in 1886, she was stored in a shed near the tunnel entrance at Gilfach Ddu and has consequently survived and can be seen at Penrhyn Castle.

Details of the workmen's train from Penscoins to Penllyn, showing the number of men picked up at each stop, the number of carriages required and the length of each train. [WSM]

— Re:- Workmen's Train —

Station	no of men	over from last station	Total	no of Carriages	Ordinary	Brake	men over		Notes.
Penllyn.	230		230	3	2	1	52		Length of Slate Run = 133 yards 1 foot (32 Cars)
Stabla.	101	52	153	2	1	1	35	3	Length of 19 Carriages @ 24 ft each
Pontrhythallt.	420	35	455	7	6	1	37		i.e:- Body 22 ft + 2 ft for Buffers = 152 yards.
Bethel.	184	37						4	The above lengths do not allow for couplings
Penscoins.	196		417	7	5	2	1		but are taken, when each Carriage or Car
Totals. =	1131			19	14	5		19	are up Buffer to Buffer.

Locomotive Fire Queen *outside its shed at Dinorwic.* [I.W. Jones]

Quarrymen about to leave Llanberis for home at the end of a day's work. [WSM]

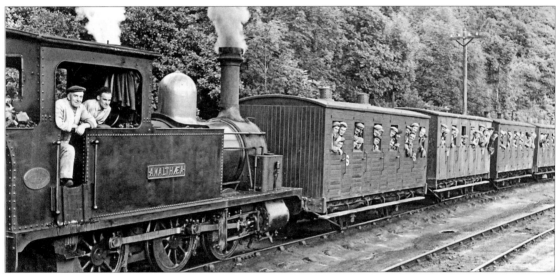

Loco Dinorwic *and the Assheton Smith's private saloon.* [Eric Lander Collection]

Some two dozen narrow-gauge railway engines operated along various galleries, hauling small wagons, of which there were many thousands, laden with rough slate to be taken to the top of an incline. Generally the inclines in use in the quarry were of a simple design and would consist of a wire rope, having a breaking point of around thirty tons, wound round a wooden drum, with one end of the wire being attached to four descending, loaded wagons while the other end would be attached to four empty wagons being hauled from the bottom of the incline on a parallel track. Sufficient momentum was created by the descending wagons to raise the empty wagons. The speed of the descending wagons was controlled by a braking system on the wire drum operated by men at the top of the incline. Most of the inclines had two tracks but four tracks running parallel were not uncommon in the quarry. At the lowest level, the slate was split and trimmed in large sheds. [GAS DQ1974]

Since the Hunslet Engine Company of Leeds had been responsible for building the very successful narrow-gauge locomotives in use at the quarry (since 1870) and the quay at Port Dinorwic (since 1898), it followed that replacement locomotives for *Fire Queen* and *Jenny Lind* were built by the same company. At a time when production at the quarry was approaching its zenith and the volume of slate being carried to Port Dinorwic was increasing, it was decided that more powerful engines were required. The first, *Dinorwic* (works number 302) a conventional 0-6-0 side-tank locomotive, was delivered in 1882 (a new copper fire box was fitted in 1899 at a cost of £96 15s 0d). She was followed in 1886 by the identical *Pandora* (works number 410 (renamed Amalthea in May 1909). A new boiler from the dry dock workshop was fitted in the *Amalthea* in December 1930 and in the *Dinorwic* in 1936. As a contingency measure, and to cover the introduction of the workmen's carriages, a third engine was ordered in 1894 which would also cover for repairs to *Dinorwic* or *Pandora* particularly during major overhauls. The third engine, *Velinheli* (works number 631) was delivered in 1895. The only difference between this and the other two was that her 3ft 6ins wheels had cast steel centres as compared to the others being wrought iron. Other dimensions applicable to all three locomotives were: wheel diameter 3ft 6ins, outside cylinders 12½ins x 20ins, wheel base 10ft, length overall 25ft 1ins, width overall 7ft 10¼ins and height to top of chimney 11ft 8¼ins. Each was capable of carrying one ton of coal and 600 gallons of water. Of the three engines, *Dinorwic* had the greatest power, but for comfort, the *Amalthea* was the favourite. *Velinheli* had the advantage over the other two when carrying out shunting work as it had the screw system similar to main-line engines that made it easier to change from forward to reverse. *Velinheli* was also considered to be the easiest to work and the fastest. [GAS XD40/10/11]

Loco Velinheli *at Llanberis.* [G. Casbeard]

A steam-hauled train would be made up of twenty trucks, each carrying four slate-laden wagons loaded by means of ramps at Gilfach Ddu, except for the last one which only had three with the fourth space reserved for the guard's hut, a total weight of 130 tons. There is an element of conjecture as to whether the same or similar method was used between 1843 and 1848 when the trucks were hauled by horses. In September 1845, work was carried out on a new railway carriage that would enable Mr Assheton Smith to visit his quarry at Llanberis and a shed was built at Penscoins the following month.

Loco Amalthea *about to leave Penscoins for Gilfach Ddu with empty wagons. [Ronald Jones]*

Although the decision to introduce steam to the railway may well have been taken by the time work started on the track in 1843, the actual specifications of the two engines *Jenny Lind* and *Fire Queen*, namely, length 18ft 2ins plus tender length 14ft 6½ins may not have been apparent when Spooner undertook the survey work. Consequently, between 1843 and August 1848, the railway accounts refer to extra costs due to 'corrections and realignment' and 'altering the curve of the railway' possibly to accommodate the long couple wheelbase of the locomotives. [GAS DQ196]

Realising the dangers attached to velocipedes, an order was placed with the Gloucester Railway Carriage Company in 1895 for fifteen carriages at £118 each and four brake carriages at £127, which were delivered within twelve weeks and were in operation by the following year.

Each carriage carried a conspicuous notice drawing the attention of the quarrymen to the conditions of travel such as 'only to be used by employees … employee must travel in numbered seat and carriage allotted to him'. Passengers had to 'avoid offensive language' and 'not to travel with infectious disease or in possession of explosives'! Each employee had to pay the foreman of the carriage in which he travels his monthly contribution which varied in accordance with the distance travelled: Penscoins, two shillings and six pence; Bethel, two shillings and three pence; Stablau and Pont Rhyddallt, one shilling and ten pence; Penllyn, one shilling and three pence. For the men residing in Anglesey, the monthly charge for travelling on the train was one shilling (5p).

In 1895, the number of men boarding was Penscoins – 196, Bethel – 184, Pontrhyddallt – 420, Stablau – 101, Penllyn – 230, making a total of 1,131. When leaving Penscoins, only three carriages were required, except on Mondays when an additional one was required to accommodate the Anglesey men. Extra carriages, with workmen already on board, were attached to the train at the respective stations. Such an arrangement was necessary because of the lack of space at Penscoins for the overnight storage of carriages.

The train left Penscoins promptly at 6 a.m. from Monday to Saturday, returning each evening

A slate laden train near Cefn Farm en route to Penscoins.
[Dave Mills]

from Gilfach Ddu at 5.30 p.m. (except Saturdays when it left Gilfach Ddu at 12.30 p.m.). During the first half of the twentieth century the engine driver was William Evans with his brother Thomas Evans of Fronheli, Felinheli as fireman.

For those who lived in Anglesey, accommodation was provided in specially-built barracks at the quarry where they could stay from Monday to midday Saturday. On arrival at Port Dinorwic and in anticipation of spending the weekend at home with their families on Anglesey, some of the quarrymen would call at the barber for a shave to remove the week's stubble.

Having spent the weekend with their families, their early departure from home armed with

The Moel-y-Don ferry, heavily laden with quarrymen returning to Anglesey after a week in Dinorwic Quarry barracks. [Len Williams]

Penscoins drum house. [Len Williams]

The braking system seen on the left hand side of the drum, controlled the speed of descending wagons on the Penscoins incline. [AC]

their ubiquitous white *walad* (sack), containing provisions for the week ahead, enabled them to catch the first available ferry. On arrival at Felinheli, often wet and cold, they headed for Penscoins where they would catch the train for Llanberis where, after leaving their *walad* at the barracks, they resumed toiling at the quarry.

Three men waited at the bottom of the Penscoins incline, unhitching the wagons from the continuous chain and safety chains and taking them a few feet to the nearby weighing platform. If the wagons were too well-oiled, they could be stopped by inserting a steel rod in a purpose-built hole in the wheel which would hold them until the wagon was ready to be dealt with. In the

Looking down the incline towards Port Dinorwic with the Halfway House fields to the right. [I.W. Jones]

Tre Newydd quarrymen's barracks at the Dinorwic Quarry Photographed taken during their renovation. [AC]

1930s, between 1,500 and 1,800 tons of slate arrived from the quarry each week which entailed weighing each wagon and counting the slates contained in groups of three (described as *mwrw* in Welsh). After counting forty-two slates, or fourteen groups of three, they were marked with a steel pin by the counting official. Odd numbers over the figure of forty-two were marked separately. Usually a wagon was loaded with one type and size of slate but when there were insufficient slates to fill a void another type or size would be used. The number, type and quality of slate was always chalked on the wagon, together with the loader's initials and the slates' point of origin in the quarry. The details were then relayed to the office clerk who recorded them in a large ledger. Similar records kept at the quarry provided the means of reconciliation if there was any discrepancy.

The weighing machine was capable of weighing up to six tons and had to be adjusted daily since its accuracy was affected by the weather. This adjustment was made by adding water to a tank until a pointer indicated the 'normal' position. Further tests for accuracy were conducted every two months by the weighing-machine makers and a certificate to this effect was kept in the office. Once the number of slates had been recorded, the wagons were hauled to the quayside by horses. In 1898, narrow-gauge steam locomotives were introduced. The wagons were taken for unloading on to the quayside with slates measuring up to 18ins x 10ins being stored between the bridge and the dry dock and the larger sizes on the sea side of the bridge.

Work on the quay, undertaken irrespective of weather, was a hard all-day slog with little remuneration in exchange for cut hands and a bad back. On rainy days, a sack draped round the shoulders provided some protection until it became saturated when it was replaced by another. Hands and clothes were protected from the sharp edges of slate by tying pieces of rubber to the hands as gloves and round the waist as an apron.

Due to the vagaries of the weather and its effect on the transport of slate by sea, mainline trucks were delivered on the port siding line to the quay where they were loaded with slate so as to be delivered promptly and safely, with fewer breakages, to any destination. Transport by rail also eliminated much of the loading and unloading which was inevitable when transport was by ship and also enabled smaller quantities of slate to be ordered by customers. With so much competition between the two systems, the cost of freight was reduced in both cases. The railway system was able to deliver directly to a specific town whereas the ships relied on delivery to ports with onward transport of the slate to its ultimate destination by whatever means available. Despite this apparent efficiency of rail over sea, recorded figures indicate that the quantity transported by the former declined between 1856 and 1863:

1856   Rail – 16,553   Ship – 66,720

1863 Rail – 6,771   Ship – 86,076

[GAS VP2880]

Where sections of the narrow-gauge railway passed over the mainline, the rails were removed between midday and 1 p.m. to allow the main line LNWR engine to bring empty trucks and collect loaded ones via the junction at Port Siding. The person responsible for this daily ritual was paid an extra five shillings per month on top of his normal wage. The empty main line trucks were left on the sloping approach to the quay enabling them to be positioned where and when required by a man riding on the back who controlled its speed by means of a foot-operated brake.

By the twentieth century, there were 130 men working regularly on the quayside, and although Welsh was the day-to-day language, many English words were in use such as 'trucks' (referring to the main line) and 'wagons' (on the narrow gauge line), 'engine' and 'incline', together with the dimension of the slates. Work was allocated between eight or nine gangs each consisting of three men. Additional workers were employed on a day-to-day basis depending on the number of ships awaiting loading. The teams, made up of a stevedore and two assistants, used special flat-bottom barrows to move the stored slate either for loading onto a railway truck or onto a ship. Since the quay workers were paid according to the weight handled (1s 7¼d per ton), wages varied considerably, depending, not only on the size of slate being handled but also on whether a ship or a truck was being loaded since a greater number of slate could be handled in the latter case. For this reason, it was the usual practice for the gangs to be moved once a month so that everyone had a change of job and location and the opportunity of improving their earnings. A similar attitude was shown to the casual workers (*hobliwr*) who sought daily work at the quay office. Work was allocated to them strictly in accordance with the list of names, without any favouritism being shown. Those over the age of seventy were however allocated lighter duties such as keeping the quay tidy and safer with discarded pieces of slate raked and collected in a special steel-sided wagon.

The larger quarry ships, such as *Enid* and *Elidir*, with their deeper holds, needed teams of five loaders compared to the normal team of three used for the smaller ships such as the *Velinheli*. A pile of slates, which varied in number depending on their size and thickness, would be placed on a plank by the man on the quay and these would slide down to the man positioned on the deck of the ship who would control both the speed and direction of the pile on their way to the hold where the third man awaited them. The remaining two members of the team were responsible for the stacking within the hold and ensuring that they were properly stowed against possible damage during the voyage.

In the 1930s, it was possible to start work on the quay as a trainee before being promoted to an apprentice if the intention was to continue working on the quay after serving his time. From a wage of 1s 6d per week earned by an apprentice, appropriate deductions were made for National Insurance stamps, enabling the worker to claim unemployment and sickness benefits.

In order that trespassing on the quay was kept to a minimum, a uniformed policeman was appointed to serve on the quay. A wooden cottage that had originally formed part of the village of huts used at the time of the construction of the Britannia Bridge was purchased in January 1850. Relocated adjacent to the entrance gate to the quay, directly opposite the quay house, it was a convenient location for the policeman to live. The quay 'police constable' in 1881 was Richard Owen.

Port Dinorwic Friendly Society

In the early part of the twentieth century, a quarryman's wages of approximately 3s 8d a day, enabled sufficient food to be bought for a family. However, this sum would be denied a man if an accident or illness occurred resulting in him being unable to work. Parish relief was more or less a 'grace and favour' situation with no guarantee of support or, if forthcoming, how much and for how long. To try and reduce the difficulties brought about by days without income, the Rev. Peter Bayley Williams of Pantafon, Llanrug wrote to Assheton Smith on 29 June 1829 requesting that a savings club or friendly society be set up 'for your quarrymen'.

> This Society (in my humble opinion) deserves every encouragement as the benefit of the members will I have no doubt be very considerable particularly in case of accidents (which are of very frequent occurrence at the Slate Quarries) and also during illness as each member is to receive 6s, 7s or 8s weekly according to the number of his family … it will relieve the Parishes considerably … as without such … the Poor would be compelled to seek Parish Relief. [GAS DQ 2632]

It was possible to submit a claim for compensation when an accident occurred but there was no guarantee that it would be paid or to what extent. The 1920-1 account book records 600 accidents and a total of £1,338 8s 6d shared between those involved with sums ranging from £1 5s to £10 15s 10d allocated. [GAS DQ 4371]

Quarrymen, by the nature of their work, were often involved in accidents or became ill because of the conditions they encountered. In an attempt to assist a family whose sole bread winner was unable to work, benefit clubs and friendly societies were formed in many Caernarfonshire towns and villages. A *clwb y cleifion* [sick people's club] was formed in 1835 on the Port Dinorwic quayside at the time when slate was being brought down Nant-y-Garth by horse-drawn wagons. Four years later, Thomas Assheton Smith granted a lease for sixty years to Edward Roberts, Vaenol Farm; David Griffith, Bryn Llanfair (Minister) and Morris Hughes, slate weigher [sic] (trustees of the Port Dinorwic Benefit Society), to enable a dwelling and club house, for the use of the society, to be built on farm land called Cae'r Dŵr. [GAS VP18] In 1842, the club house was leased to *Cymdeithas Gynorthwyol Porthladd Dinorwic* when

Dinorwic Friendly Society badge. [Gethin O. Jones]

it was formed and registered within the Friendly Society Act as the Port Dinorwic Friendly Society. In 1845, the society, known locally as *Clwb Siloh*, recorded amounts paid out to members and the reason for the payments: '1862 paid to bury Thomas Williams, Singrig £3 11s 0d; paid to bury David Jones, Aberpwll £7 16s 0p; paid to bury William Roberts, Aber £8; 17 March 1863 paid to bury Morris Hughes £7.' The last entry shown in the book was on 9 June 1866. [GAS XM 166/80; XM 94/1; UWB BP MS622]

Although the club did not confine membership exclusively to quarrymen, it was having financial problems by 1887 as indicated in an auditor's report which stated that the contributions being made by the members were too low:

> It was all very well for some to join at age 30 plus but not at the same rate of contributions as made by those who joined from the age of 15 plus. A graduated scale is therefore recommended i.e. the older you are when you join the more they pay otherwise it is an injustice to the younger members. It is only that the sickness have [sic] been reasonable that the Society has been able to continue.

Griffith Jones, the secretary, recorded that in 1889 there had been 170 members in 1884 but this had decreased to 144 by 1889 due to deaths and resignations. The cash in hand was reported to be £254 17s 5d in 1884–5 and four years later £344 8s 0d. Mr Assheton Smith, possibly as honorary member of the club, subscribed £5 annually to the funds.

The club house was leased to the club by the Faenol estate until 26 September 1899. A letter of 1897 pointed out that it was in a state of disrepair and that the dilapidation was causing serious concern.

The latter years may well have been a worry to the officials because of falling membership and the state of the building, half of which was used by the club and half by a caretaker. As a result, the decision was taken to approach both the Oddfellows and Foresters in the hope that one or the other would take over the society, but they declined due to lack of funds and the members being too old and a decision was taken to continue as long as possible.

3: The Port of Dinorwic

The question of expanding the dockside and the provision of additional storage space had been a matter of contention for many years. Since the greater part of Felinheli was owned and controlled by Lord Boston (until 1889 when most of it was sold to Assheton Smith) very little, if any, development could take place on the south side of the inlet without his approval. Even so, Thomas Wright, one of Thomas Assheton Smith's partners at the Dinorwic Quarry, wrote in 1792 stating:

> He (Boston's agent) promised to let us have part of Lord Boston's property near the salt mill for the use of the slate quarries and I met his agent there (at the quay) and staked a part for that purpose … The Slate Quarries go on very busy. Slate cannot possibly be brought down fast enough to answer demand. I have a scheme of making a new road from the quarries which if you approve of when you see it may possibly be carried on and enable us better to supply the demand for slate. [GAS VP2562]

Having been granted permission by Boston for the quay to be extended, Thomas wrote twelve months later:

> Have been yesterday at Moel-y-Don quay the wall of the same is finished only wanting some more Ballast and Rubbage [sic] to back it and I likewise agreed with them for to erect a Bridge at Salt Mill and make a low wall from the bridge to the quay and want a little timber to keep the vessels from the quay and have also set up proper fasts of Timber and Rings am sure you'll like the quay and bridge when you see them I think I can pay all the expence [sic] about the quay etc under £24. [UWB Porth-yr-Aur 29084, 29240]

In 1802, three additional berths were built within the inlet at Aberpwll, between the point where the old mill had been located and the present bridge which crosses from one side of the harbour to the other. [GAS DQ 3464] Irrespective of the number of improvements made to the wharfs within the 'mud estuary' as it was described on contemporary maps, only small schooners could be accommodated for loading and unloading. Larger vessels were unable to come alongside a wharf due to lack of water and the time-consuming method of lightering from the Moel-y-don jetty continued.

Frank Oswell, the civil engineer who was involved in the new harbour (1902 Paper 3296) stated:

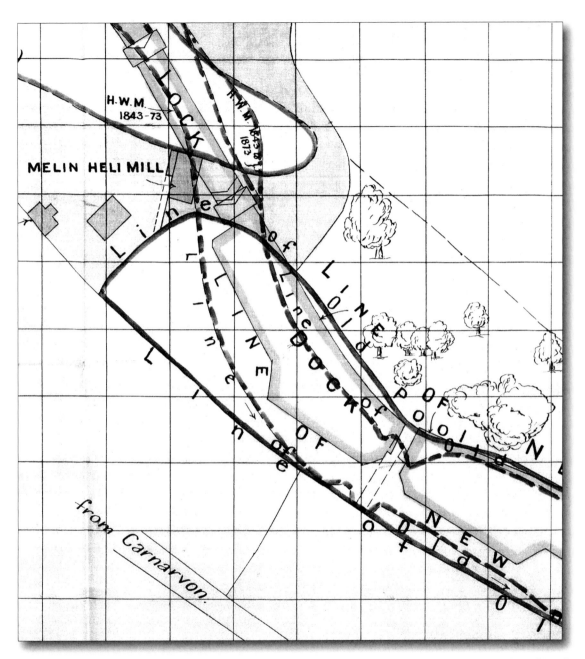

Site of the old mill in relation to the original pool and the present dock. [GAS]

Port Dinorwic was formerly called Felinheli, meaning 'sea-water mill'. From a mill that existed there about a century ago which is said to have been worked by the tides presumably by impounding the flood-water and using it as the tide fell. The foundations of the mill were found in the course of the present work at the site indicated in old estate plans. The inner part of the creek was the little more than a marsh with a stream [Afon Heilyn] trickling through it. Part of the foreshore near the mouth was reclaimed and converted into a quay and a tidal dock in 1797 by walls of roughly squared limestone laid without mortar and backed in the roughest-hewn slate slabs, 5 inches to 10 inches in thickness and as much as 11 feet or 12 feet in length. Later on the dock was continued up the creek with walls of similar construction to a point near the entrance of the present dry dock. The old quays were for the most part made ... of such loose materials as slate rubbish, sea sand, copper dross (from the old mines at Amlwch) and rough stones.

By the time Thomas Assheton Smith II had inherited the Vaynol estate in 1828, the name of the village was being quoted as Port Dinorwic rather than Felinheli because of its slate quarrying connection. Improvements to the wharfage continued with the building of a 'new pier' between 5 December 1833 and 1 July 1834 at a cost of £370 10s 0d. [GAS VP4378] A 'new quay', built between 23 November 1839 and 12 January 1841, facilitated not only the storage and dispatch of slate from Port Dinorwic, but also allowed larger ships to tie-up alongside. [UWB Porth-yr-Aur 29092]

Between 1820 and 1845, extant records relating to the export of slate to America refer to the point of loading by lightering as 'Moel-y-Don' even though earlier in the century it was being referred to as 'Velin Heli' (NWG 20.3.1817)

Slate storage and difficulties with wharfage continued to be a problem until Lord Boston agreed in 1889 to sell all of his property in Llanfairisgaer, including the quay, to the Faenol estate. [GAS VP2379) (see Chapter 5 – Shops, Trades and Houses]

New Harbour, 1898–1900

As the end of the nineteenth century approached and the demand for slate continued to grow, G.W.D. Assheton Smith decided to rebuild the harbour at Port Dinorwic so as to facilitate the loading and unloading of ships within a lock-gate system.

On 10 April 1897, a construction agreement was signed with Philip Ayres of Ayres & Company. This, the largest undertaking for the port (including lock gates built by Cleghorn and Wilkinson, Engineers, Northwich) cost £18,527. When work started on 26 March 1897, Afon Heilyn, which normally flowed into the inlet, was contained within a wooden trough built on the Bangor side of the eventual harbour, thus enabling it to flow to the open sea without inhibiting work on the harbour.

Many conditions were incorporated into the 1897 contract including the contractor having to provide a temporary bridge of timber or other material 'capable of opening readily', the operation not requiring more than three minutes to allow vessels to pass in and out. The bridge had to be 'sufficiently substantial to bear safely the moving load of a train of slate trucks in the roughest weather'. It would also be necessary to build a temporary dam against the incoming tide and 'existing telephone, gas and water pipes relaid in a trench' in the new dock.

Facing: The plan of the wharf in 1856 gives an indication of how little space there was for storage of slate.
[GAS]

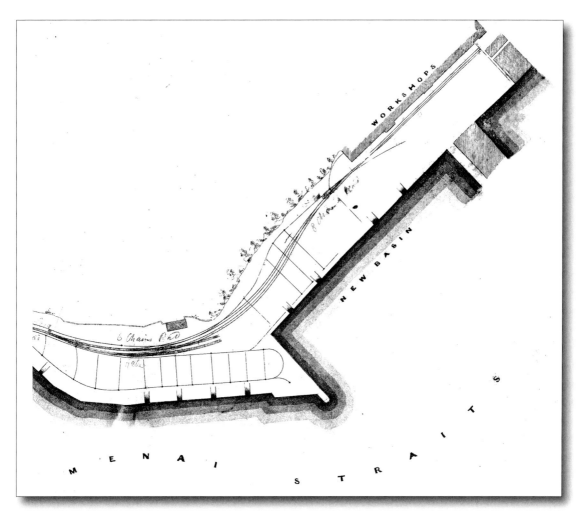

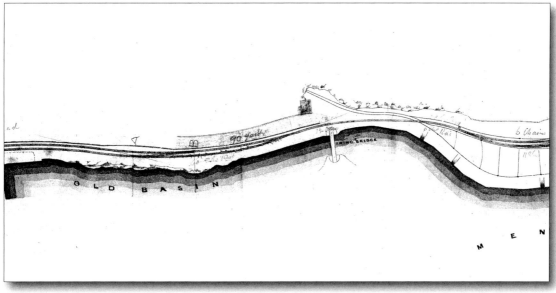

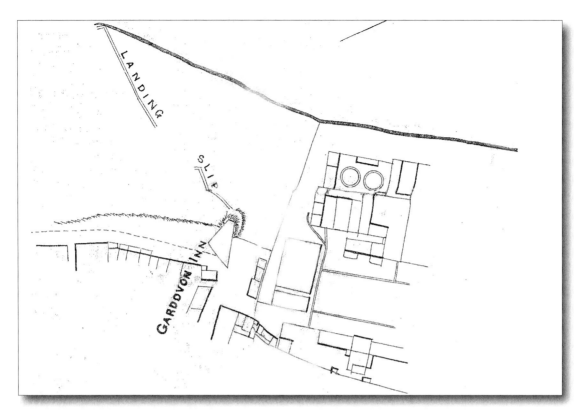

Sketch map showing the position of the old jetty at the bottom of Snowdon Street. The circular buildings on the right are the gas works. [UWB]

*Shipping inside the old harbour (*hen gei*) at Port Dinorwic, c.1885.*
L–R May Fly, Duke of York, Jane Ann and Helen & Ernest. [Glyn Pritchard]

Schooners Jane Grey *and* Esther *at the old dock, with Plas Newydd in the background. The narrow entrance must have caused some difficulties with entry and exit as well as restricting the size of vessels that could use the dock. [Dr Hugh Roberts]*

A number of schooners inside the old harbour c.1895. [AC]

Due to the size of the old harbour c.1890, larger steam vessels were confined to the outer wharfs. [AC]

The contract also stated:

The Dry Dock: The walls are of concrete 11 feet in thickness at floor-level. Two Gwynne centrifugal pumps, one 13-inch and one-8-inch area capable of delivering together nearly 5,000 gallons per minute enable the water within the dry dock to be discharged when the gate is closed. When a ship is at the dry dock for repairs it rests on three-foot high keel-blocks spaced along the dock floor and with the ship supported on each side by timber logs. The entrance is closed by a steel falling-gate hinged at the bottom.

It was reported that whilst preparatory work was in progress 'in all parts even deep in the blue clay were found the remains of oak and other trees some of them oak logs being still quite sound although they must have lain there for many centuries. A hard clay-shale found on the north side of the dry-dock was strongly impregnated with copper and was believed to overlie rich ore'. The masonry was of limestone from Traeth Bychan, a quarry in Anglesey.

Work on the harbour began in April 1897 and the contract was completed within the specified time resulting in the new harbour being opened on 10 September 1900. [GAS VP2763, 2764, 2379]

The Elizabeth Bennett *discharging ballast by means of the chute prior to entering the dock for a cargo of slate, 1906. [GAS]*

The old bridge across the Afon Heilyn. [Eric Lander Collection]

The old bridge in the course of being demolished with the quay offices in the background.
[Emyr Wyn Roberts]

Contractors—MESSRS. AYRES & CO.

CERTIFICATE No. 3 (Supplementary) For Month ending June 30 ___ 1897

DESCRIPTION.	WORK DONE.				PREVIOUSLY CERTIF'D. Cert° N°2.			AMOUNT DUE	
		£	s.	d.	£	s.	d.	£	s.
Port Dinorwic —									
Part Re-construction of Harbour —									
Dam across entrance, on a/c.		900	0	0	257	10	0	642	10
Footbridge across Dock, on a/c.		16	10	0	5	0	0	11	10
Value of remainder of work done to date (see Cert° N°3)		877	5	6	664	12	0	212	13
Total value of work done to date £		1,793	15	6	927	2	0	866	13
Less, 10% for Retention		179	7	6	92	14	0	86	13
		1,614	8	0	834	8	0	780	0
Materials on ground, at 75% market value. All as in Cert° N°3.		302	17	0	397	8	0	less 94	11
Total sums due on a/c. up to June 30 —		1,917	5	0	1,231	16	0	685	9
Paid up to June 30 (Cert° N°3).		1,697	13	0	1,231	16	0	465	17
Due on a/c. of Supplementary Cert° N°3. £								219	12

Costs relating to the reconstruction of the new harbour at Port Dinorwic. [GAS]

Whilst the construction of the new harbour was taking place, the Afon Heilyn was diverted directly to the Menai Strait along a wooden trough. [GAS]

A variety of steam-powered machines used during the construction of the new dock. [Eric Lander Collection]

The first ship to be loaded after the opening was (no doubt by arrangement) the SS *Vaynol*. [GAS XM5583]

The dry-dock technicians worked closely with their counterparts at the Dinorwic Quarry workshops at Gilfach Ddu, Llanberis – a reciprocal arrangement which worked extremely well over the years. Repairs were not confined to ships belonging to the Dinorwic Quarry Company. Any vessel, provided it did not exceed approximately 160 feet in length, could be accommodated in the dry-dock (the only such facility between south Wales and Birkenhead). According to the 1911 records kept by E.E. Neele, Coppack's ships from Connah's Quay were regularly surveyed and overhauled there. Other ships mentioned were the SS *Lincolnshire* which had extensive repairs carried out to the engine room and the SS *Briton* which had a new funnel fitted. Invariably, whilst a ship was in dry-dock, the opportunity would be taken to clean the hull and, if necessary, apply a fresh coat of paint as was the case with the 145-foot SS *Bangor*, belonging to the Anglesey Shipping Company, which required 'two coats of black varnish amounting to 27 gallons and "boot-topping" which required 65 lbs for the first coat 53 lbs for the second'. The SS *Penrhyn* had a new 'scotch' boiler measuring 13ft x 10ins with three furnaces and smoke-box fitted at a cost of £2,830 in 1920, and she was followed shortly afterwards by the old steamer *Panmure* that required a new propeller fitted. As far as the ship's crew were concerned, dry docking a ship was unpopular as it meant a cut in pay or even being signed off for the duration of the repairs.

During the two world wars, many ships made use of the dry-dock facilities at Felinheli. Although the equipment available was antiquated and caused the work to take longer than would be the case in other shipyards, the expertise was there to tackle most tasks. The site had the advantage of being partly concealed from marauding enemy aircraft which were seen or heard from time to time over the village but their presence would be more by accident than design.

A number of vessels damaged by enemy action had to be repaired during the Second World War including: HMT *Achievable* (November 1941); HMV *St John* (September 1941 – June 1942

The new dock walls under construction. The dam that was built to prevent the sea encroaching can be seen on the far right. [Eric Lander Collection]

The general scene during the construction of the new dock with the walls nearing completion. Note the steam-powered crane operating on railway lines along the dockside. [Eric Lander Collection]

The walls of the dry dock have been completed. [Eric Lander Collection]

Above and below: The lock gates have been installed. [Eric Lander Collection]

Vessel in the dry dock for repairs, November 1911. [W. Wyn Roberts]

SS Velinheli *and another vessel in the dry dock. [AC]*

and November 1942 – November 1943): The work on HMT *En Avant* (fitting Krupp 3-inch gun, depth charge throwers etc.) took from October 1942 to March 1943; HM *Drifter* (November 1944); HMT *Sheldon*; HMY *Ottowa* (September 1941); NFS Fire Boat *Seafire* (March 1944); MTBs 719, 709, 713, 709 and LCI (L) 351.

Utilities

The gas was produced on the quay near the old tidal dock in 1860 and used for lighting in offices, places of worship, the homes of estate officials as well as street lighting both in the village and on the quay. As far as the remainder of the houses and shops in the village were concerned, candles and paraffin lamps continued to be the normal form of illumination. When production of gas ceased in 1893, although electricity was still in its infancy especially as far as domestic use was concerned, enquiries began to be made by the Vaynol estate regarding the installation of a generator at the quay to supply electricity to the nearby offices and homes of estate officials, and another in Vaynol park, near to the mansion, for use by the Assheton Smith family. A number of companies were asked to submit quotations and plans for equipment, as well as laying a mains cable from the power house at the dry-dock complex, in order that street lighting could be installed. Belshaw & Company were awarded a contract in 1896 and P.R. Jackson & Co. Ltd., of Manchester for the installation of street lighting in the village, at a total cost of £7,212 5s 3d. [GAS VP3201] A letter written in 1917 described the electrical generators at the dry-dock power house as 'two Willan Steam Set directly coupled to two compound machines together with motor boosters and a set of chloride batteries for storing the electricity'. Steam was produced by Galloway hand-fired boilers until they were replaced by an anthracite-fired gas plant which proved to be very unreliable and it was necessary to have a diesel engine on standby. The gas

One of the Dinorwic steam ships in the dock c.1930. *Note the slates stacked on the quayside. The General Manager's house in the distance. [AC]*

Below left: Slate being loaded on to main line trucks. [AC] Below right: Loco No. 1 *(also known as* Lady Joan *for a short period) on the quay in 1950. She was transferred to the quarry in 1964. [Ronald Jones]*

Below: The scene on the new quayside c.1905. *The loco is being driven by William Evans. Note the electric lighting in place. [AC]*

Slates on the quayside awaiting dispatch. [John Lloyd]

Two schooners await high tide and the opening of the lock gate c.1905. [Len Williams]

Left: Dry dock workers. [AC]

Below: The cottage, situated opposite the quay house, used from 1850 by the quay policeman. [AC]

By the 1920s, schooners had been replaced by steam-powered vessels. [Len Williams]

Above left: SS Vaynol being loaded with slate at the old harbour in 1896. [GAS]
Above right: Slate being loaded in the same way c.1920. [AC]

The Assheton Smith's yacht, SY Amalthea, in the dry dock c.1910. This vessel was lost on New Year's Eve 1918 when, as HMS Iolaire, she was ferrying demobilised troops home to the Hebrides. Over 200 men lost their lives in the worst British maritime disaster since the loss of the Titanic. [AC]

Aerial photograph of the new dock, the dry dock, quayside and the old harbour, taken c.1941 by an RAF photographic reconnaissance aircraft. [GAS]

plant was also very dangerous and produced an objectionable smell. The Vaynol generator for charging batteries was powered by a pressure gas engine of 100hp and which also proved to be potentially dangerous.

By 1909, when gas was still being used in adjoining towns, seventeen electric street lamps had been installed in the village at strategic points such as the corner of Port and Terfyn Terrace, the post office, the top of Snowdon Street, Menai Street, Old Sail room, the bottom of Allt Gam near the railway bridge, the bottom of Brynffynnon Road, Caernarfon Road (opposite the Toll House near St Mary's Church), Menai View and Bryn Alun. [GAS DQ3591, 3596]

Each street lamp was independently controlled and had to be visited each evening to be switched on with the aid of a long pole (as had been the case with gas lamps), by individuals such as Twm Morgan, Griffith Owen, Bob Parry and Guto Jones with each person being paid one

Quay harbour master William Morris (centre) and family. [Jean Elias]

Dry dock workshop. [Bethan Smith]

shilling (5p) per month for the daily ritual whether it was oil or electric street lamps. This process had to be repeated each morning in order to switch the lights off.

By 1918, electrical power had been extended to Vaynol officials living at Ffinfa, Fronheli, Bodarwy, Bodarborth, Dock Cottage, Vron, Nantadda, Bryntirion Lodge as well as Port Church, Siloh Chapel, Tan-y-Graig and Halfway Inn together with sixty-eight other houses and shops in the village. When W.E. Parker of Dinas applied to be connected on 7 November 1917, the reply stated 'regret it is impossible under present [wartime] conditions to entertain your proposals [to supply electrical power]'. Eleven years later, Tan-y-Maes and Dinas were still dependant upon oil lamps according to the Llanfairisgaer Parish Council minute even though Parker had offered the sum of £12 towards the cost of installing electric street lighting.

Since batteries charged by direct current generators only had a certain holding capacity, the electricity supply intended for lighting purposes was unable to cope when other electrical appliances such as kettles, irons and electric fires began to be used, especially in the evenings when demand was at its greatest. The gradual dimming of light continued until such time as the generator was restarted in order to maintain the supply. If there was a possibility of an apparatus causing extra demand on the electrical supply, it was expected that permission would be sought by the owner before installation took place.

Such was the lack of expertise in the early days of electricity and of individuals able to deal with possible problems that, when the local electrician received his enlistment papers for the forces on 21 June 1916, T. Lloyd Williams, the general manager, wrote to the appropriate authority 'William Williams … [is] the only man capable of attending to the electric light plant which supplies my works and also the town'. A further letter on 16 April 1917 read 'my electrician William Williams, Snowdon Street, Port Dinorwic [is] to appear before the Gwyrfai Local Tribunal

Canadian Vickers
Motor Launches
(built by Elco in
New Jersey in
1915/16) in Port
Dinorwic dock
1917.
[John Hughes]

as the man is indispensable to me I wish to appeal for his exemption from military service'. The result of the appeal is not recorded.

Mr A.R. Glover, who had served his apprenticeship with Lever Brothers, Port Sunlight followed by a period with the Caernarfon Light Works near Victoria Docks, was appointed electrician in February 1918 'at £3 per week with house and a reasonable supply of coal and light … to work under Mr Pritchard'. When Mr Glover eventually took charge of the power station, he also became responsible for all new installations by wiring from the main cable in the road. He was also responsible for the reading of meters every three months in order that bills could be issued for the electricity used. Those who did not pay on time or after a couple of reminders, would have their supply cut off by Mr Glover on the instructions of T. Lloyd Williams, general manager. [GAS VP3204]

For those without the benefit of an electrical supply, power for radios was provided by means of a wet battery which had to be recharged periodically at a cost of around two shillings (10p) a time, either at a local garage or a shop specialising in radio equipment. The private electric supply first generated in 1901, came to an end on 31 August 1934 when it became the responsibility of North Wales Power Company. As a result of the change from the old system of direct current (DC) to alternating current (AC), householders who were fortunate enough to have electric irons, kettles or other electrical appliances used under the direct current system, had them changed free of charge by North Wales Power.

When F.O. Harper, city electrical engineer at Bangor gave an address on 12 April 1947 at Aberystwyth on the subject 'North Wales Resources', he made the following comments:

> North Wales has never had ample and cheap supply of electricity and has suffered accordingly … It is ironical that while North Wales has all the essentials for cheap electricity in its Water and Tidal Resources it is compelled by the Electricity Acts to purchase its electricity at a cost which is probably the highest in Britain. [GAS VP2379, 2764, 3201, 3204, 3596]

4: The Village

After the main line railway had been built between Bangor and Caernarfon in 1852, and traffic had been diverted from passing along Augusta Street (see Transport chapter for additional details), Lord Boston, who owned most of the land within the parish of Llanfairisgaer, began releasing building plots (c.1853) in the area generally described as Garddfon, which extended from Augusta Place to the Garddfon Inn near the ferry jetty. Contemporary rate books provide such details as the name of the owner, the leaseholder and of the tenant of each property but with the address being shown collectively as Garddfon. [UWB BP1149 (1852)] This continued until individual street names began to appear such as Snowdon Street, New Street (later renamed Menai Street) and Beach Row (later changed to Beach Road).

At this time, there were no planning regulations to control the type of house or shop that could or could not be built. Properties appeared where there was a vacant plot and in accordance with the lease holder or builder's capital (a house or shop could be built for approximately £200). Ground rent, being dependent on the size of the property, usually varied between 18s and £1 per annum. Most of the houses in this area were expected to have insurance cover of approximately £100.

In anticipation of properties being built on Bush farmland, a new farm house (described as Bush *Newydd* or New Bush in Rate books) and outbuildings were built on nearby elevated ground c.1869. The 1871 census recorded the occupant of the relocated farm as being Thomas Jones, (aged 52). Subsequently, the old farm buildings that straddled the toll road were demolished which effectively released eighty-seven acres of farm land for development extending down to the shore. Houses, interspaced with shops, were built usually in groups of two, three or more, along the toll road until most of the land had been taken up.

Assheton Smith's frustration in not being able to develop the quay and adjacent land to his liking, ended in 1889, when Lord Boston agreed to sell him all his property in Llanfairisgaer, described as being from and including 'Bush farm towards a cottage called the Taproom' together with the Garddfon Tavern and the property Terfyn, for the sum of £15,330. [UWB Lligwy Papers 1083, Bangor MSS 1191]

Mr & Mrs Jones, Bush Farm, c.1900. [AC]

Bangor Street. A high-class general store on the corner of Terfyn Terrace and Port Terrace in 1887, later the premises of Lloyds Bank. [AC]

J.T. Jones (1816–87) and his wife, Jane, lived in the property called Terfyn, located where Terfyn Terrace was later built by him and W.B. Buckingham. When employed by Assheton Smith as a joiner, Jones and his wife lived at Four Crosses (also known as Rhiwal), and later at Fronheli. As a result of being appointed Manager of Works at the quay, they lived at Plas Dinorwic (the 1871 census describes him as a 'ship owner'). When he resigned his post in 1872, the family moved to 8 Frondeg Terrace (later renamed Terfyn Terrace).

Many of the houses in the village at the turn of the century were very basic in their furnishings since the occupants would, more often than not, be too poor for any extravagance and ostentation. Such simple furnishings were obtainable locally from the Arvonia and similar shops in the style required and at an affordable price. Blinds would be seen on windows rather than curtains and floors covered in linoleum rather than carpet. Even as late as the 1930s there were a few houses in Felinheli that still had uncovered soil floors.

Life for most women, at least for those without the benefit of domestic servants was hard with the drudgery of housework and the washing of clothes without the aid of modern facilities. Clothes were often boiled in a cauldron in an outhouse or shed before then being put through a hand-operated mangle to extract the excess water before being hung out to dry if sufficient space was available. When space was restricted or even unavailable, houses had to contend with drying the clothes indoors which resulted in an atmosphere of damp and condensation that was hardly conducive to good health.

An indicator of the first efforts to provide a regulated water supply appears in a letter, dated

7 April 1885, from Lynde & Son, civil engineers of Manchester which refers to the 'Bush Spring Scheme' and the construction of a twenty-feet diameter reservoir capable of holding 20,000 gallons of water, at a cost of £550. On its completion four months later, the company advised J. Henry Thomas at the Carnarvon Union offices that, since 'several springs having been tapped and led into the Port Dinorwic sewer, there will be no occasion to provide water for flushing purposes'. It can only be deduced that some form of sewerage system had been installed, but no information is provided as to its location or extent. The possibility is that since most of the initial building work had taken place adjacent to Snowdon Street that the sewer had been built along its length and down to the sea shore where its content was discharged. [GAS XM5727/39]

Five years later, at a meeting of the Caernarvon Sanitary Authority, it was stated that a report had been received by Dr Rees, the Medical Officer of Health, complaining about the lack of fresh drinking water at Port Dinorwic. Although little information is available on the subject the legacy of £2,000 left by a Mrs Mary Thompson of Terfyn Terrace in 1901 intended for the provision of a fresh water scheme in the village appears to have resulted in taps being provided at various points. Each house wishing to participate received a key to operate the tap at an annual cost of 10d. Alternatively, fresh water could also be collected from springs at various points in the village.

Individuals living in Beach Road preferred to carry water from a spring near Dinas which purported to have beneficial medicinal properties. This was also the source of fresh water for visiting schooners. For those living in the vicinity of Nant Cottage at the bottom of Nant-y-garth, water had to be carried, two buckets at a time, from a pipe near the Afon Heilyn. Hand pumps were also found in a few places such as Dinas, Brynwaen and Glanrafon. To supplement water needs and reduce the quantity that had to be carried, large slate cisterns were constructed at the Dinas slate yard and installed in many houses as a means of collecting rain water.

In the case of the spring near the Arvon Tavern, where the flow of water varied from time to time, it was decided that it should be collected in a tank and a tap provided to facilitate ease of

Port Terrace. The YMCA was established in the first house on the left hand side. [AC]

Dinas slate yard workers. [W. Wyn Roberts]

access. The same provision was to be made at the bottom of Allt Gam and at Pant Dyrus.

Prior to a public sewerage system being installed in the village, each house had its toilet, usually called the *tŷ bach*, located in the back garden. This earth closet was emptied periodically on to a dump in the garden and covered daily by ash from the grate and other household refuse. This was collected period-ically by means of horse and cart and taken to one of the farms in the Tan-y-Maes area where untreated it was spread on to the fields. Such a service could only be accomplished if there was access for the horse and cart to the back of a house. Where this was not possible, it was up to each tenant to deal with the disposal as best they could.

The Sanitation Committee of the Llanfairisgaer Parish Council reported on 21 April 1931 that there was a need to improve sanitation at Augusta Place and Menai Street and 'that water toilets were required in the houses at Beach Road and Glan-y-Mor Road'. The only way that the emptying of earth closets could be accomplished from these properties was by carrying it through the house and emptying it onto the shore at Pant Dyrus a few yards in front of the houses. This section of shore became such an eyesore as a general dumping ground that in 1929 the Parish Council decided that it was to be cleaned before the forthcoming regatta.

Complaints were also being voiced in the 1930s regarding the absence of water closets at Tai

Bangor Street. The approaching coal cart was owned by Owen Roberts of the Arvon Tavern. [AC]

Railings, Dinorwic Terrace and Pink Terrace. Gwyrfai Rural District Council was asked to 'provide the same sanitary arrangements as had been carried out at Augusta Place' although no records survive as to exactly what the 'sanitary arrangements' were. Overall the question of converting from earth closets to water closets was dependent on a number of factors including the availability of nearby water mains, whether the owner of the property was willing for the conversion to be made and that the tenant was willing for the work to be carried out. This resulted in conversions being made haphazardly with no specific council plan. As far as general rubbish was concerned John Owen, Garreg Llwyd was appointed in 1931 to do the work of 'public scavenging' twice a month at a cost of £169 per annum and for the refuse to be carted by 'motor lorry' to Cae Metta. It was specifically mentioned that no tins were to be deposited on the beach as they were also being 'carted to Cae Metta'.

Subsequent to an investigation being made as to the feasibility of using Marchlyn Bach lake for supplying (fresh) water to the villages within the Gwyrfai Rural District Council area, including Port Dinorwic, a report was published in October 1931 stating that the lake was eminently suitable in all respects for the area mentioned. Although estimated to cost £30,000, the scheme was recommended and it was anticipated that it would solve many of the problems being experienced at Port Dinorwic and other villages within the area. [GAS VP7017, 7020]

Postal services

John Jones, who ran the Halfway House shop, was appointed sub-postmaster on 9 August 1841, the first in the area. He held this position until November 1869 when he was dismissed for 'money order irregularities and the bad way in which the office duties had been conducted'. He was replaced by Richard Cadwaladr Griffith and the opportunity was taken to relocate the post office temporarily to a shop known as Vaynol House at the top of Snowdon Street. As the properties were being built in the direction of Bangor, they were numbered accordingly. On 12 January 1873, Griffith, who was also a qualified chemist, entered into a ninety-year lease, at an annual rent of £3 18s 0d, on two adjacent properties described as the Medical Hall and the Post Office, sited next door to Elim Wesleyan chapel. [GAS VP1292] As a result of its relocation and the building of properties along Bangor Street having been completed, no doubt at the instigation of the General Post Office (GPO), the decision was taken to renumber the properties by commencing at the top of Port Terrace, along Bangor Street and ending at the terrace called Menai Hill near to the (then) railway bridge.

With the introduction of a public telephone system by the GPO early in the twentieth century, it was decided that an application be submitted to the Bangor postmaster for a 'Public Telephone call office to be made available in the district'. When the system was installed at the Port Dinorwic post office in the 1930s the postmaster had, in

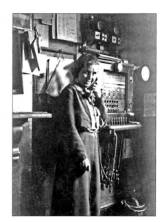

Nancy Williams operating the local telephone exchange in the 1930s.
[Kathleen W. Roberts]

addition to dealing with normal postal work, the task of operating the switchboard. When first introduced, telephones were mostly used by business people in the early 1930s as the list of names shows: 1 – Post Office; 3 – Hen Station slate work; 4 – Menai Stores; 5 – Dr Hennessey; 6 – Roberts & Sons; 7 – local garage; 14 – J. Henry Jones; 18 – Vaynol Estate Office; 22 – Dinorwic Quarries and 36 – Dr H. Edwards.

All the telephone calls were timed by the operator by means of a clock located above the exchange board. There was no time limit for local calls but for every long distance, or trunk call a ticket was made out showing the caller's name and telephone number together with the time taken for the call. All the tickets were then sorted into compartments in a special box and taken to Bangor Post Office where the cost of the calls was calculated and bills for the subscribers compiled. This system was still in use until after the Second World War. For those without the benefit of a telephone, the alternative was communicating by telegram. The arrival of a telegram was greeted with a sense of foreboding and trepidation, especially during war-time.

Inns

Apart from the Halfway House Inn, according to the 1883 edition of *Slater's Trade Directory*, the village had a further four licensed properties to choose from: the Garddfon Inn which according to a ninety-nine year lease between Lord Boston and John Thomas in 1812 relating to a plot of ground stated: 'Thomas erected a dwelling house thereon which eventually became the Garddfon Inn'. [GAS Henry Rumsey Williams 980 12 November 1827] However, there is a reference to the

Garddfon innkeeper, Grace Griffiths, being involved with road maintenance in 1792. [UWB Porth-yr-Aur 3426] It is possible that both dates are correct since the earlier date may refer to a building near to the jetty whilst the latter date refers to a newly-built nearby property which became the Garddfon Inn. Little information is available on the Arvon tavern located on the Caernarfon road

The Halfway House Inn with Margaret Ann Roberts and her nephew John Williams in the doorway. [Michael Roberts]

The Halfway House Inn c.1950. The right-hand side of the building, not visible in the photograph above, was once a general store. [R.G. Wilson Roberts]

Bangor Street. On the right are a newsagent's shop, a butcher's shop and Manchester House. Note the old- and new-style street lights. [Len Williams]

except that it was in existence in 1839 and continued as a licensed property until *c*.1890. The Britannia Vaults, at the top of Snowdon Street, had a chequered existence subsequent to being a licensed property. An attempt at renewing its licence in October 1888 was refused and an appeal reported that 'Mr Allason said that the appellant was dead and that therefore the appeal must fall through. The bench concurred'. The fifth and youngest licensed property, the Victoria Hotel, was built in 1863 and licensed the following year. [GAS XQA/1/9/90]

Wholesale suppliers
The rapid growth in the number of shopping outlets in Felinheli during the second half of the nineteenth century, linked closely to an increasing population, created the need for a reliable method of replenishing stock when necessary. Goods destined for the area originated mostly in Liverpool, a city closely connected with north Wales. David Jones established a successful business at Llandderfel in the 1850s selling a wide range of goods as well as dispensing simple drugs. He later founded David Jones & Company in Liverpool with the intention of developing the market along the north Wales coast. To this effect, he used the shipping company of Robert Owen, trading as the Aberdovey & Barmouth Steamship Company, vessels such as *Christiana*, *Telephone*, *Rebecca Countess of Lisburne* for the conveyance of supplies. Such was the regularity of *Christiana's* visits to the port with her diverse cargo from Liverpool that Lake's of Caernarfon arranged for goods destined for Port Dinorwic shops to be left by *Christiana* at the shed, known as *'Sied Christiana'*, rather than be taken to Caernarfon and returned by road.

In an attempt to increase the number of outlets and expedite deliveries, David Jones & Co. introduced steam traction engines (manufactured by Fodens of Sandbach) on to north Wales's roads in 1912. Called Dreadnoughts, these had a carrying capacity of three tons and were dark

The small shed (nearest the sea) was used for storing supplies brought by the SS Christiana *until required by local shops.* [John Lloyd]

green in colour until 1918 when its livery was changed to yellow to enable various advertise-ments to be displayed promin-ently on the side. These engines were never popular when being driven through towns and villages due to the smoke created and the occasional trail of red hot cinders left along the streets.

Trades and Shops

The number of traders established in Port Dinorwic by 1868 was recorded as four bakers, one bookseller, four boot and shoe makers, two butchers, one chemist and druggist, one flour dealer, two grocers and tea dealers, one linen and woollen dealer, four marine stores, one clog maker, two braziers and one blacksmith. During the remaining years of the nineteenth century, the number of shops increased significantly.

Although still at school, William Ellis Thomas was apprenticed to Owen Morgan who had a shop at Berw House at the top of Port Terrace for half-a-day per week to learn the tailoring trade. When he completed his training, he worked for a while in Liverpool until deciding to apply for a job as a cutter with J.V. Williams at Manchester House, Port Dinorwic which, at that time, dealt in both provisions and cloth. When Liverpool House became vacant *c.*1930, Thomas seized the opportunity to buy it and started his own tailoring business. His employees, including Robert Roberts who specialised in jackets and trousers for thirty years, worked cross-legged on a table with the stitching done mostly by hand, but occasionally by machine. Suits for the Vaynol keepers were made alternatively by W.E. Thomas and John Rowlands, another tailor in the village. A matching cap to the suit was made by sending a piece of material to a specialist firm called Try & Lillie in Hanover Street, Liverpool. When Mr Parker, the head game keeper at Vaynol, required a suit it would be made from Harris Tweed. A navy-blue serge suit would also be made for the quay policeman with buttons bearing the letters DQ (Dinorwic Quarry) sewn on by a local woman. Such a suit would cost £5 10s 0d as compared to corduroy trousers which cost 9s 6d.

Gypsies would call to order a suit when passing through the village and this would be sent to a pre-determined destination along the coast with pay-

Gwyrfai Jones, chemist (previously the premises of William Jones, baker) and the village Post Office. [Rhian Gwyn]

ment unfailingly made. Such reliability in paying for garments did not extend to some individuals in the village who required months to pay off their debts. When one such individual who owed W.E. Thomas for three suits, came in to order one in a very thin material, he was told in no uncertain terms that it would be so thin that he would not be able to see it! The village tailors not only made suits as required, they also carried out alterations. When Sir Charles Assheton Smith had finished with his suits, rather than discard them he would have them altered for the benefit of one of his employees.

Not all the tailors in the village had the benefit of a shop window. Some, like John Henry Thomas living at Rhianfa, John Williams of Augusta Place and Robert Williams of Llys Myfyr operated at home where rolls of cloth in different patterns and colours were available from which the customer could choose. Every suit was handmade. At times of bereavement, mourning suits and dresses were produced within a matter of days even when the tailors operated on their own. 'Going-away' outfits for young brides were made as readily as men's suits.

In addition to the tailors, the village also boasted a number of dressmakers and others adept with needle and thread. Two such dressmakers who lived in Tan-y-Maes were as capable of producing a dress or frock for everyday use as they were for special occasions, whether it was for a wedding or bereavement. Tuition was also available in the art of dressmaking from Miss Jones who had a shop next door to Menai Stores.

Amongst the many boot and shoe repairers, there was one in particular whose shop was a popular venue for village elders to meet for a chat. William Owen, a man with a bad limp but who

Bangor Street c.1930. The first four properties on the right were the post office, a chemist's shop, a tailor's shop and grocery shop. [Len Williams]

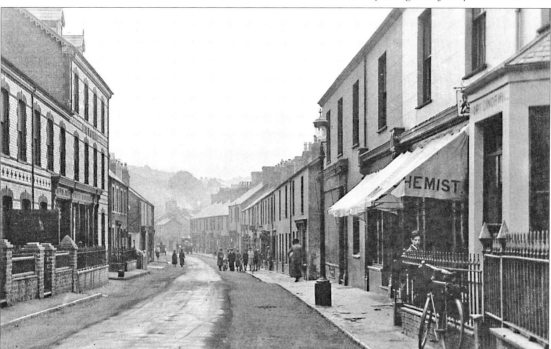

nevertheless walked each day from his home in Brynwaen, carried out his trade in a small lock-up shop in Bangor Street. The place, dimly lit by a paraffin lamp hung from the ceiling directly above his head, was untidy with pieces of leather scattered about, either waiting to be used or having been discarded. Apart from William Owen's own chair, there were additional seats for the members of the local 'parliament' who daily came to discuss the latest in local gossip or more profound matters of the world which had been gleaned from visiting seafarers, the newspapers and, in later years, from the radio. William Owen did not contribute a great deal to the discussion, since his lips invariably held a number of nails ready for dispatch into the boot or shoe in hand. Sometimes on a Friday night, a child was permitted to accompany his or her grandfather on condition that it would contribute nothing but listen to everything.

Another debating group would gather at Michael Williams' smithy on Beach Road where they would not only have a lively discussion but also the benefit of seeing his skilled hands forming wrought iron work as well as repairing farm implements and ship's parts. Much of the railings and gates seen in the village and the local cemetery were made by him. Sometimes a visitor suffering from warts would come to dip their hands in his cooling water with its purported medicinal benefit.

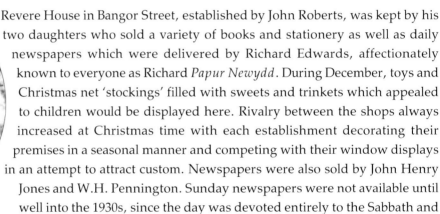

Michael Williams

Revere House in Bangor Street, established by John Roberts, was kept by his two daughters who sold a variety of books and stationery as well as daily newspapers which were delivered by Richard Edwards, affectionately known to everyone as Richard *Papur Newydd*. During December, toys and Christmas net 'stockings' filled with sweets and trinkets which appealed to children would be displayed here. Rivalry between the shops always increased at Christmas time with each establishment decorating their premises in a seasonal manner and competing with their window displays in an attempt to attract custom. Newspapers were also sold by John Henry Jones and W.H. Pennington. Sunday newspapers were not available until well into the 1930s, since the day was devoted entirely to the Sabbath and spiritual matters; profane matters of the outside world had to wait until Monday.

A number of the shops sold sweets which have always attracted the child with a sweet tooth and Miss Lloyd's shop (later kept by Mrs Edwards) on Menai Hill, was no exception. The child, used to a very simple and basic life without a great deal of embellishments, would find the various shops in the village fascinating places as he or she accompanied the mother on a shopping expedition. As far as toys were concerned, many of the children in the village would have to be content with window shopping since the limited income of most families would not cover such luxuries.

Many of the items on sale would be displayed, not only in the shop window, but also outside where rows of poultry and game would be seen. With labour being so cheap, it was not unusual for thirty assistants to be employed in a small shop and they had to deal with the display of goods, cleaning and in the delivery of goods to customers as well as serving.

H.N. Bank was a versatile individual who traded at Greenwich House, 71 Bangor Street not only as a jeweller, watch and clock maker, but also as an optician and an agent for the sale of

Premier, Raleigh, Rudge, Whitworth and other cycles. He was as adept at repairing these as he was in dealing with the delicate mechanism of a watch. Bank would also undertake to maintain and wind clocks in churches, chapels and private houses. In 1905, he gave an undertaking to 'the mending, cleaning, regulating and weekly winding of the Vaynol Hall household clocks at a cost of £5 5s 0d per annum'. [GAS VP2399]

Many establishments carried as good a range, variety and quality of goods sale as any shop in Bangor or Caernarfon. The shop kept by Richard Owen on the corner of Terfyn Terrace and Port Terrace was only small, but the specialist groceries that he sold, including snails, preserved ginger, olives, cheeses, chutneys, spices and sausages, inevitably attracted a certain clientele, including the Vaynol family. The property was purchased by Lloyds Bank Ltd in 1897 subsequent to taking over the bank of Williams & Company (described as the Caernarfon Old Bank) which had been established at the village in 1886. By 1903 the branch was open every Tuesday from 10.30 a.m. to 2.30 p.m. and in 1939 it become a full branch, opening daily from 10 a.m. to 3 p.m. and Saturdays from 9 a.m. to 12 midday.

The Temperance Café in Felinheli, with its well-known confectionery and home cooked meats, was well patronised even by people from Bangor and Caernarfon. Such was its reputation that wedding receptions were also held there occasionally.

Both Manchester House (which later had the benefit of a glass canopy outside the shop to protect the displayed wares) and Dinorwic House (kept by J.V. Williams and David Evans) respectively had a reputation for quality and service. In addition to selling groceries on a retail basis, David Evans also sold certain items wholesale, such as flour. A popular item which he sold, especially with children, was treacle and this he dispensed out of a large cask into a tin can. Other grocery shops such as Assheton House and Bangor House, although smaller, still enjoyed a good reputation. With such competition, it was imperative that those in business, when making their own purchases, spread their support amongst a number of shops rather than concentrating on any one in particular if they expected patronage to be reciprocated.

In 1908, after a period at sea serving as steward and cook, Richard Williams (1868–1946), together with his wife and daughter, Eunice, established a shop called Menai Stores that supplied grocery and general provisions. Having the benefit of maritime connections, in addition to supplying local needs, he also delivered supplies to ships in the harbour by means of a large wicker basket measuring 6ft by 4ft by 2ft carried on a hand cart. His son, after a period learning the trade with Morris & Jones in Liverpool, joined his father in the shop circa 1925.

Although most shops had the advantage of a cool cellar where goods were stored until required, perishable goods, such as meats and bacon, had to be sold in a fresh state soon after an animal had been killed or, in the case of fish, soon after it was caught, especially in warmer weather when deterioration occurred at a faster rate. If the intention was to keep meat for any length of time then it had to be cured. Sticky paper was to be seen in abundance hanging from the ceiling in an attempt at killing flies which were always a problem with food on open display. Many of the shops had the benefit of a window shade or canopy to alleviate to a certain degree the effect of the sun on displayed goods. Rice, flour, tea and similar products were supplied by the wholesaler in large quantities which had to be weighed and packaged by the retailer into smaller saleable quantities. Similarly, cheeses and lard were cut with the aid of wire attached to a wooden board in accordance with the weight or even the price specified by the customer.

Compared to present day opening hours of 'eight till late' or even twenty-four hours, most shops in the village were open from eight in the morning until the same time in the evening. Even though shops were closed for the obligatory half-day on Thursdays, it was in fact the day for the young assistant to visit customers and collect orders in time for them to be made up for delivery by bicycle on the following day.

Friday would see the shop open until nine-thirty in the evening and even later on a Saturday when people from nearby villages came for their week's shopping and a spot of gossiping. This sort of service was expected and had to be given by shopkeepers if patronage was expected since there was so much competition from similar establishments. Once the shops had closed on Saturday evenings and the last customer departed, irrespective of the late hour, the keepers and assistants headed for the barber's shop for a shave in anticipation of attending chapel or church the following day. Although the main street through Felinheli was a hive of activity from Monday to Saturday, not a sound would be heard on a Sunday except for the toll of the church bell which would be a reminder of the day for everyone irrespective of faith or denomination.

Established initially as a taxidermist at Mona House in Snowdon Street, Thomas Francis moved to Bangor Street where he became established as a barber. His shop had an interesting array of guns together with knives, bayonets, rifles and revolvers, also powder and shot pouches dating back to the Boer and First World War, all displayed on the walls. No one dared touch any of the items; inspection was limited to sight only. Nevertheless it relieved the time spent waiting while customers had their hair cut and possibly a shave.

John Henry Jones (1878-1934), having served his time as a monumental mason (he was responsible for all the gravestones at Llanfairisgaer cemetery bearing his trade mark 'clasped hands' symbol), had a shop at 84 Bangor Street that sold stationery, tobacco, cigars, postcards, china and fancy goods. In addition, his interest in photography, at a time when few had such aspirations, resulted in First World War soldiers when home on leave, calling at his small shop to have their photograph taken in uniform. As a result of being asked to print various items such as bereavement cards, he purchased a small machine. This proved so successful that the printing

enterprise was eventually transferred to Dinorwic House when the property became vacant, and eventually taken over by Richard Francis Jones, John Henry Jones's son. In addition to their business acumen, John Henry Jones and his children were all accomplished musicians.

Richie Francis Jones in his printing works at Dinorwic House. [Bethan Smith]

Vodol House sold linoleum covers, clothing, drapery and other haberdashery products and was a large enough shop to have a number of assistants, together with a lady cashier in her own office where cash from the counter was delivered with the aid of pneumatic tubes. Apprentice milliners and saleswomen were taken on from time to time, such as Elin Richard of 1 Marine Terrace, Criccieth who was employed on 1 March 1899 at a salary of £1 5s 0d per month. A similar agreement was made for Thomas Davies of Meirion House, Criccieth who was 'desirous of acquiring a practical knowledge of the trade of draper' and was taken on for a four-year apprenticeship on 20 May 1895. Conditions written into the agreement were that he 'will not absent himself without the express permission of Richard Pritchard [the proprietor] ... [who] will provide Thomas Davies with good and sufficient meat and drink at his table and as one of the family ... also suitable and sufficient clothes [also] medicine, medical attendance [and] pocket money.' [GAS XD19/98-100]

Vodol House with Mrs Jones (the owner) and Katie Smith (Singrig) in the doorway. [Len Williams]

William Jones built many of the properties along the main street of the village including those from Dinorwic House up to and including the Wesleyan chapel, Elim. He also built his own shop Arvonia, the largest shop in the village, on the opposite side of the street. He was also responsible for building a row of fifteen houses, described as 'working class houses', from Arvonia in the direction of Bangor and known as Mona Terrace. [GAS VP6938] Arvonia, established by 1883, compared favourably both in size and range of goods, with shops in Bangor and Caernarfon. In addition to selling most articles required for setting up a home, it also catered for both the farming and shipping industries. William Jones was assisted in the shop by his son Roger, and daughter Annie, a philanthropic and altruistic individual by nature who cared greatly for those in need, both physically and academically. She was known to leave money anonymously with shop-keepers when she became aware of an impoverished family in need of food. Christmas time was the opportunity for her to continue her good work by distributing gifts, especially in the form of good reading books, to a number of village children. William Jones, his son and daughter, and his housekeeper, Miss Davies, lived in a flat above the shop. He died in 1901, aged 56.

Although bread was available in many shops, a number of housewives preferred to make their own dough which was baked at the nearest *tŷ popty* (bakery) where it was taken wrapped in white linen cloth. Since there were many who had their loaves baked in a similar fashion, a numbered tag was applied so that the loaf could be readily identified.

William Jones' bakery was at Bryn Morfydd, Bangor Street where he was assisted by R.D. Vaughan, Richard Watkins and Gwilym Jones (who later started his own bakery business at the old sail loft on Beach Road in the 1930s). In addition to shop sales, bread and cakes were also

Arvonia with a very basic display of items being sold in the shop. William Jones, the proprietor, and an assistant are standing in the doorway. [AC]

carried in a large basket to be sold from house to house. When William Jones died, the business was taken over by Watkin Parry until it became a cake shop for a short period kept by Oswald Jones. Next door to Bryn Morfydd was the small Clynnog House café run by Mrs Mary Jones. In October 1931, she applied for an explosives licence which was apparently required in order for her to sell fire-works.

Butchers' shops were well represented in the village including that of Owen Roberts at 25 Bangor Street. One of his sons, Thomas Roberts, after serving his time as a butcher on a White Star liner, decided to 'come ashore' in about 1924, by which time his father had decided to retire. Thomas Roberts took over a small bake house, previously occupied by James Morrison in Snowdon Street, where he produced pork products such as hams, bacon and pies. By 1929, having successfully established himself by delivering produce around the countryside in a small van, he invited his three sons, William Elidir Roberts, Owen Glyn Roberts and Evan Owen Roberts, although established in their respective trades, to join him. From Snowdon Street, he moved to Bangor Street to a double-fronted shop, previously occupied by the butcher, John Jones, thus allowing his products to be better displayed. Of the two individuals holding a licence to slaughter animals in 1931, one was R. Jones, (trading as R. Jones & Sons) in a building (built in 1873) at the bottom of Snowdon Street and the other was Thomas Roberts & Sons at Dinas. By this stage, the company was known simply as Roberts & Sons, and had a greatly increased range and quantity of products. It now concentrated more on the wholesale rather

than retail side of the business and their fleet of vans, displaying the 'laughing pig' emblem, delivered to a number of outlets in north Wales.

Amongst the properties in Snowdon Street was a shop called Cinallt whose owner had the assistance of a multi-coloured parrot who would call 'Shop!' each time a customer entered. In addition to the fish sold at the corner shop opposite Arvonia, pickled herrings could be bought from a house in Augusta Place. Before Tommy Jones started his barber shop near the garage, the place was kept by Mr and Mrs Horlock as a fish and chip shop. Next door to Thomas Francis the barber shop (75 Bangor Street), was Eiffel Café owned by Grace Williams and her

William Jones, baker and confectioner. [Len Williams]

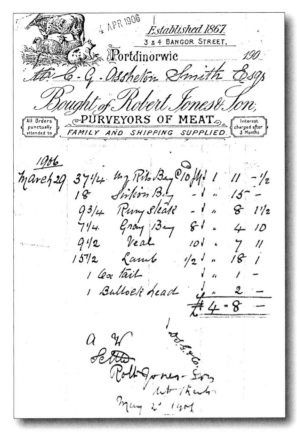

Thomas Roberts with family and employees at the Dinas factory. [W. Wyn Roberts]

Roberts & Sons, butchers, Commer delivery lorry. [W. Wyn Roberts]

Robert Jones & Son, butchers - receipt dated 1906. [GAS]

brother, Robert, known as *Bob mul* because he kept a mule for hauling his coal wagon, passenger trap or even the village hearse. Next to his shop was the Victoria Vaults, followed by a butcher shop specialising in pork and inevitably known as *siop porky*. This later become a shoe shop, then a barber shop. The shop next door was run by a woman who, despite making delicious home-made bread bore the misleading and inappropriate name of *Betsy Bara Caled* (hard bread). On the other side of the road at Efrog House lived John Owen Roberts or John Owen, Llanddwyn as he was known to many, who sold coal and operated a haulage business with the aid of a horse and cart which were housed in a yard adjoining his house. He also conveyed commercial travellers selling tea and other products to shops in and around the village. He was one of the first people in the village to own a car which he used for his taxi business.

Bessie Pierce preparing pies at Roberts & Sons. [W. Wyn Roberts]

Moriah Chapel, Bangor Street on the left. The electric street light was installed c.1905. [Bethan Smith]

The community living in Brynffynnon Road and nearby properties in Tan-y-Maes was well served by a variety of shops both large and small. Not only did Seaview Terrace have the benefit of a small grocery shop, shoes and boots were repaired a few doors away. Robert Owen living in nearby Helen Terrace, made use of his front room for selling fresh meat and other provisions. A daily visit to nearby Cambrian Bakery for fresh bread would complete the daily shopping without the necessity of having to walk down to the village. Miss Sally Morris's small shop on Brynffynnon Road sold postage stamps in addition to general provisions. A short distance down the road was an establishment run by Mr and Mrs William Owen known as *siop Fawr* (large shop). Although less than a mile from the main village, it stocked a large selection of household items as well as general provisions.

Although few people lived in Siloh and Aberpwll, they were nevertheless well served by a variety of itinerant tradesmen including Charlie Bertorelli from Caernarfon who came selling ice cream from an adapted motorbike and sidecar. Eagerly anticipating his arrival every Friday evening in the summer time, the children would come along for a 1d ice-cream cornet as soon as he appeared. Cockles were sold by a man from Newborough from a horse-drawn cart twice a week, who announced his arrival by shouting at the top of his voice. A Mr Edwards from Penrhosgarnedd sold bread brought by means of a horse-drawn van with brass lamps on each side. Another tradesman, Caradog from Ty'n Coed, Nant-y-Garth was the provider of milk which he dispensed by means of ½ pint and 1 pint measuring cans from a churn carried on a horse-drawn cart. Hugh Roberts also delivered coal by the same method, whilst paraffin, the other essential product used daily by all the houses, was delivered by lorry every Tuesday by Jack Davies from Llanfairpwll.

Interspersed amongst the established village shops were numerous houses partly given over to selling one or two products, either to produce the only income or to supplement a meagre wage. Paraffin, used for lighting and heating, was a popular commodity available from a number of sources in the village. Some were sufficiently enterprising to collect and sell bundles of firewood for a penny or two. Vegetables, grown in small gardens or allotments were also sold alongside fish caught in the Strait or a rabbit or two which had 'accidentally' caught itself in a snare.

In addition to their normal chores, farmers also undertook a daily milk round with the aid of a horse-drawn cart or float. A measured quantity of milk from the churn was dispensed directly into jugs produced by the housewives. The milk retailers in the 1930s (by which time bottled milk had been introduced) and later were: Griffith, Bryn Farm; Dafydd Edwards, Penrallt; John Jones, Bush Farm; Harry Jones, Carreg Coch; Rowlands, Tan-y-Maes; Hughes, Garth Farm; Thomas, Ty'n y Coed Dairy; Edwards, Vodol Uchaf; Robert Hughes, Vodol; Hugh Owen, Garth and Owen Jones, Cefn Coed. Horses were so familiar with the route that instructions between owner and horse were minimal. However, any instructions were ignored completely when the horse became aware that a snack of stale crusts awaited his pleasure at certain houses.

Anglesey smallholders were also involved in selling farm produce, in particular eggs, butter and poultry that were brought across on the ferry to be sold either on a stall near the ferry hut or in a nearby lock-up shop which now forms part of the Garddfon Inn. One such smallholder was Mrs Jane Hughes of Llanddaniel who dressed in a Dickensian manner with heavy black garments and a large black hat. She would travel from her home to Moel-y-don by means of a donkey-drawn cart and, after unloading her produce onto the ferry, the donkey would be unharnessed and allowed to roam and forage until her return in the evening when she would be heard calling his name. William Jones from Brynsiencyn also brought both milk and vegetables across on the ferry for selling from a hand cart which he pushed from house to house.

Robin cocos would entice housewives to buy his cockles and herrings from a handcart by shouting at the top of his voice. Another person from Brynwaen also relied on a handcart for selling paraffin and vegetables. Nellie Kelly sold soap and pegs from a basket which she carried from house to house, whereas Harry Hughes sold firewood by pony and trap.

Itinerants, such as Mr and Mrs Hamilton from Bangor, visited most houses – he mending umbrellas while she kept her eyes open for any coconut matting that needed repairing. Knife grinders were as familiar

Robert Hughes, Vodol Ganol (third from the left) with family and friends.

Hugh Roberts, coal merchant. [Les Harris]

as the onion sellers with their wares hanging from a pole or draped on a bicycle. Colourful Romany gypsies travelling by horse-drawn caravans together with a pony or two trailing behind were no hindrance on the road in the early part of the century since most traffic would be travelling at the same pace.

Tramps, travelling as they did from workhouse to workhouse, were also part of the scene. Their needs were simple: a little hot water and a crust from a friendly householder assisted them on their way to their next favourite watering hole. Scottie, as his name would indicate, was from Scotland but he had spent most of his years in the Caernarfon area. His favourite place for sleeping was the brickworks in Caernarfon where he would be assured of warmth, however cold the night. He preferred this to the regimentation and discipline of the workhouse.

Although the language of the village was primarily Welsh, paradoxically, most of the shops had the English word 'House' added after a certain name such as Liverpool House, Manchester House, Windsor House etc. The Memorial Hall was invariably referred to as the 'Hall' even when the conversation was in Welsh. Many of the street advertisements were in Welsh: 'The Ace Steel

Bangor Street, 1906. The first two shops on the left were those of Robert Jones, butcher, and Menai Stores. [AC]

Bicycle' seen near the old Arvon tavern on Caernarfon Road became 'Y Beisigl sy'n ddur i gyd' Since there were only a few who were completely fluent in both English and Welsh, it was imperative that certain notices were bilingual. A warning notice on the railway, for example, would read 'Rhybudd – Cosbir Troseddwyr' alongside its English equivalent 'Notice – Trespassers will be prosecuted.' Bilingualism seemed to be higher amongst women rather than men due to their work as domestic servants with English-speaking families. It was usually the case that the better-off members of the community had one or more domestic servants or maids.

A catalogue and programme published in September 1925 in connection with a grand bazaar in Vaynol Park to raise money towards the erection of a war memorial, showed a variety of interesting advertisements including:

Robert Williams with his horse-drawn taxi. He and his sister ran a café in Bangor Street. [Mona Thomas]

Mrs D. Evans, Dinorwic House Golden Stream Tea; William Jones of Arvonia Ironmongery Stores - kitchen ranges, iron and brass bedsteads, kitchen and dairy utensils, mangles and washing machines, farm and garden implements, household requisites, paints (Goodlass' Bird Brand), oils, varnishes etc; W.D. Jones, garage, agent for all leading makes of cars , motor cycles, cycles from £3 5s 0d, all makes of tyres in stock, taxis day or night, wireless sets and accessories; J. Henry Jones, was described as a 'Music and General Printer, stationer, etc., and selling tobaccos, cigars, postcards, china and fancy goods as well as being a

Gwilym Jones, Menai Bakery. [Harry Wyn Jones]

Menai Bakery at the old sail loft on Beach Road. [Harry Wyn Jones]

Houses overlooking Dinas shipyard. [W. Wyn and Helen Roberts]

photographic and wireless dealer'; Owen R. Williams, Drug Stores sold products described as 'The Elfrida Toilet Preparations are delightful aids to beauty and they will certainly charm you and give you charm'; Misses N. and A. Thomas, Fronheulog, Port Dinorwic 'High Class Confectioners and tea rooms, Wedding, Birthday and Christening Cakes made to order, Tobacco and Cigarettes, Chocolates, Sweets and Ice'; E.M. Williams, Bangor House, confectioner, grocer and provisions dealer'; Morris Utility Stores, 18 Brynffynnon Road sold hardware, confectionery, art wallpapers, paints, varnishes and distempers ; John Thomas, Rhianfa, Ladies' and Gents' Tailoring; John Rowlands, Windsor House, 'suits to measure at cut prices, agent for EM-AR rain-coats, hats, caps, ties in latest shades and styles, men's under-wear and hosiery, boots and shoes, quarrymen's nail boots at cash prices;' W. Jones, Bryn Morfydd, baker and flour dealer, high class confectioner, supplied fresh bread daily; Hugh Roberts of Frondirion, coal and coke merchant, haulage contractor; David Evans, Dinorwic House a tea dealer, family grocer, provisions merchant, corn and flour dealer; M. Roberts, Vaynol House, high class tobacconist, chocolates, sweets and biscuits of every description; Evan Henry Lewis, 82a Bangor Street, electrical and mechanical engineer etc. electrical work on motor cars a speciality, magnetos and dynamos overhauls, private plant installed; Kate Jones and Son, Menai Hill, coal and coke merchant est.1873.

J. Henry Jones, printer and stationer.

Soon after the turn of the twentieth century all the spaces left between groups of houses were used to store coal by one of eight merchants since every property without exception had need of coal. Conveniently, with the introduction of motor cars, the last space to be occupied was that of the Central Garage. By the time most of the building work had been completed, Tower Terrace, Railway Terrace and Mona Terrace were collectively renamed as Bangor Street.

The following figures give an indication of the growth and decline both of the population and premises in the village:

Year	Population	Houses	Shops
1803	225	45	
1831	530		
1848	750		9 (1850)
1861	1450	281	11 (1858)
1871	1900	473	42 (1868)
1881	2020	519	64
1901	2160	537	74
1921	1880		
1931	1840		
1951	1780		
1961	1810	648	38

5: Social Care

Before the turn of the nineteenth century, those living in the two hamlets of Aberpwll and Tan-y-Maes were almost exclusively employed in agriculture. Consequently, most of the families were poor and many were dependent on parish relief in times of economic hardship. Parish records reveal the payments being made in the late eighteenth century:

> 26 February 1778 it was agreed with Griffith Jones to take in Mary Williams being with child and having sworn her settlement on the parish till she is brought to bed at 2d per week'.
>
> 31 October 1781 it was agreed to give Margaret Jones the wife of John Roberts ten shillings and 6d to save her bed (that is to say) to pay her rent this half year ending All Saints and no more that 2s 6d a fortnight as per vestry … that 2s 6d per fortnight be allowed to Margaret Jones ye wife of John Roberts who left her on this parish with three small children and the sycamore tree in Churchyard be cut down to be sold for ye use of the parish and another stump useless to be sold ye same way.
>
> 1788 at a vestry held at the Parish Church of Llanfairisgaer it hath been unanimously agreed between us whose names are hereunto subscribed to allow James Rowlands pauper four shillings a week whenever necessity requires it.

The question of income for those living in Aberpwll was alleviated to a certain extent when slate began to be brought from Fachwen by horse and cart along the Nant-y-Garth road built down to the port in 1812. The situation was further improved in 1824 when the quarry railroad was built. Gradually, as the quantity of slate being brought from Llanberis to Felinheli increased, so did the number of people being employed.

Following the passing of the 1834 Poor Law Act, relief for the poor, which had previously been administered largely through the parish vestry, was taken over by a Board of Guardians enabling those without any means of financial support to be able to apply for assistance so that, in theory, a destitute person could be given tokens that could be exchanged for food and/or clothing. However, it was no easy task to obtain such relief since the Board expected that any 'luxury' item within the household would first be disposed of to raise money before an application would be considered. As late as the 1940s, the Relieving Officer would call to distribute assistance to the needy at the Conservative Club and a house on Brynfynnon Road which was called *tŷ talu* (paying house).

The Relieving Officer would obtain tenders from shopkeepers to supply food and wearing apparel to applicants in exchange for tokens. Specified shops would then be authorised to deal with such tokens pre-printed with a list of foods and clothing, when presented by a claimant.

These tokens, which could not under any circumstance be exchanged for cash, were then presented by the shop keeper to the clerk for payment.

When an applicant, who was unknown to the Board, applied for assistance the clerk would usually pay a visit to the applicant's home to visually assess its contents in order that he could brief members of the Board about his findings and, in particular, confirm suitability for assistance. Even when members of the Board were sympathetic to the plight of the applicant, they were governed in the amount that they could distribute by the sum allocated to them from the local poor rates. As far as many families were concerned, applying for parish relief would only be done as a last resort; they would prefer to earn a little money by taking in washing or similar tasks rather than endure the humiliation of asking for relief.

Even when a member of the family was in employment, wages would often barely cover their needs and it was often necessary for the wife to carry out domestic service to supplement the income. Although this entailed getting out of a poor house to carry out duties amongst the better off, the revelation and comparison seldom created envy or bitterness. More often than not it was beneficial since she would be earning a small wage and quite often receiving discarded clothes for herself and family use. These additional duties, carried out stoically even when in poor health, were appreciated by the children who, in most cases, realised the sacrifice that the parents were making on their behalf. Even the children would be encouraged to seek occasional employment, such as making deliveries for one of the shops, if only to provide a little pocket money for themselves.

To assist in the administration of the various parishes, they were grouped into unions and the Caernarfon Union was made up of twelve parishes extending from Clynnog to Bangor and inland to Llanberis, together with five Anglesey parishes in the Newborough area which had historical and economic connections with Caernarfon. The third requirement was that institutions or workhouses were to be made available by these unions for the care of the paupers and homeless. The Caernarfon Union workhouse was located on the site of the present day Eryri Hospital.

The Llanbeblig workhouse, which had been in existence prior to the passing of the Poor Law was, because of its poor standard of cleanliness and other reasons, eventually replaced by a new building in Caernarfon in 1846, but only after a great deal of pressure was applied on the Board of Guardians to comply with the law. By contrast, according to the *Carnarvon and Denbigh Herald* for 13 January 1883, special fare had been prepared for the previous Christmas consisting of: 'roast beef, plum pudding and $5^1/2$ gallons of beer. A Christmas tree was provided together with some presents for the inmates'. [GAS XG/2/131, XG/2/134, XG/2/144, XG/2/188]

Where there were industrial developments, housing became a problem since there was a tendency to build small, cheap houses close together without the benefit of basic facilities. The development of the slate industry and its ancillary works in Bangor and Caernarfon, for example, exacerbated an existing problem of the lack of suitable accommodation for the families. Inevitably, such overcrowding and close proximity of the houses enabled any disease that broke out to travel rapidly and infect many. When epidemics such as smallpox and typhus occurred, the Carnarvonshire & Anglesey Infirmary in Bangor (opened as the Loyal Dispensary in 1810) came under a great deal of pressure. To ensure that some relief was provided, the workhouse and empty houses were also used to treat the sick.

The epidemic of cholera in Caernarfon in 1865-6 caused Sir Llewellyn Turner to write to the Secretary of State on the 9 March 1866:

> … that the (Board of) Guardians should be requested forthwith for a Fever Hospital and that the fever patients be removed and their dwelling thoroughly cleansed and their old filthy bedding destroyed and fresh bedding supplied this fever has now lasted about five months and that there are numerous dens in the town which ought to be closed being quite unfit for human habitation.

The Assheton Smiths of Vaynol often acted in a philanthropic manner by making contributions towards easing the suffering of the sick and poor. In 1884, the sum of £5 was shared between thirty people in sums of between 1s and 6s including, for some reason, one person receiving 10s 6d for the purchase of a bottle of port wine and another sufficient moneys to purchase a pair of blankets. At a time when deer were culled in Vaynol, soup made from parts of the animal, was distributed to the poor of the village. Further assistance was given during the winter as was reported in the *North Wales Chronicle* on 9 February 1892, 'Mr Assheton Smith, Vaynol Park has this season again according to his Annual Custom generously forwarded a gift of half a ton of coal to all deserving poor of Port Dinorwic and neighbourhood'. Vegetables and fruit grown on the estate were also distributed to both the poor and local hospitals. There were other benefactors in the village such as Miss Annie Jones of the Arvonia shop, who would quietly assist those in need.

Illness and Treatment

When illness occurred, treatment for the patient was governed entirely by cost and availability. Until surgeries were established in the village during the nineteenth century, treatment was usually sought from the local druggist or even a shopkeeper who sold a variety of purported cures. According to various trade directories, the first chemist and druggist in Felinheli was John W. Jones in 1868, followed by Richard Cadwaladr Griffith. By the twentieth century, the qualified chemists were named as G.H. Jones, MPS (1910) and R.A. Evans, MPS (1913). In the 1930s, Gwyrfai Jones, MPS took over the shop previously occupied by the baker William Jones.

Dr Owen Thomas Jones, MRCS, the son of John Thomas Jones and his wife Jane (see Shops, Trades and Houses chapter), received his medical training at St Bartholomew's Hospital in London. He established his practice at 6 Terfyn Terrace in 1873 whilst living at 5 Terfyn Terrace. Other doctors listed in the trade directories of the latter part of the nineteenth century were Dr Henry Edwards, Dr A.H. Jacob and Dr Hennessey.

Dr Henry Edwards (1866–1921) qualified at Edinburgh University Medical School in 1895. His first surgery was in a room above the Temperance Café in 1897. He married the following year by which time, he had built a house called Trefeddyg at the bottom of station

Dr Henry Edwards [Dr Henry Edwards]

hill. Patients living in outlying farms and villages were visited by means of a pony and trap irrespective of the time of day or the weather, until he acquired a Ford Model T car. When a patient living on Anglesey required his services, he would cross the strait by means of the ferry. Following his death, his widow ran the practice with locums of varying competence and sobriety until she sold the practice to Dr Hennessey.

Ford Model T car (CC1140) registered 2 October 1914, owned by Dr Henry Edwards, parked outside the surgery with the chauffeur in attendance.

Mrs Margaret Ann Williams, a midwife living in Snowdon Street in the 1920s, was also liable to be called out at any time. She could be summoned by opening her front door, which was always unlocked, and knocking on the side of a cupboard. Her area covered the village and outlying district. Although small in stature, she would visit her patients, walking the lonely roads on her own whatever the weather, without fear.

Mrs Gracie Williams or Nurse Mobey (her maiden name) as she was generally known, came to Port Dinorwic in 1933 having been trained in general nursing and midwifery at Christchurch Hospital, London and nursing practice in Plastow. Although regarded at her initial interview (held at the YMCA and chaired by Canon Ben Jones) as being too young, within a week of arriving, and whilst acting as relief midwife, she delivered a baby at Penmachno, her first unsupervised delivery. By the time she retired she had delivered over 300 babies in the village.

If residents experienced dental problems, the initial reaction was to seek treatment with a doctor or chemist, both of whom were capable of extracting teeth. Dr Edwards charged 1s to extract without an injection and 2s 6d with but it was not unknown for a patient to change his or her mind half-way through the attempt, pleading for pain relief even if it cost more. By the 1930s, the service of a dentist, Mr R. Richards, was available at Clynnog House between five and seven o'clock on Wednesday evenings, to take care of any toothache or similar problem.

Dr Robert Owen

Another name synonymous with medicine was Robert Owen. He started his working life on the family farm at Tan-y-Maes before deciding to study medicine. He studied at Anderson's College of Medicine, Glasgow during 1871–3 (winter sessions) and Glasgow University 1870–2 (summer sessions). Having failed one part of the examination, he returned to the village where he took on the role of a druggist, dispensing medicines to the sick, initially at the shop next door to the post office. Later, as the result of being asked to vacate the property by Richard Cadwaladr Griffith, the sub postmaster who required it for Hugh Griffith, a member of his family and a chemist

Dr Robert Owen and his son, William John Owen, who qualified as a chemist in 1916

apprentice, 'Dr' Owen continued as a druggist in a small shop called Springfield, at the top of Snowdon Street.

After successfully retaking his medical exam and qualifying as a doctor, his name and qualifications appear in the *Medical Register and Medical Directory* with the qualifications LRCP, LRCS, LFPS 1892. In addition to listing his qualifications, the 1926 *Medical Directory* also provides the following information: St Mungo's & Anderson College, Glasgow; Med. Off & Pub. Vacc. Nᵒ· 1 Llandwrog Dist. Carnarvon Union; Med. Ref. Pruden. & Other Assur. Cos.; Member BMA.

Between 1891 and 1892 Robert Owen, together with his wife Ellen and four children, lived at 6 Warnock Street, Glasgow, possibly when he was involved with St Mungo's and Anderson College.

Although fully qualified as a doctor, rather than establish a surgery he appears to have continued with his previous role as a druggist. When his twenty-eight year old daughter, Mary Owen, was a supplementary teacher at the Council School in 1912 her address was given as 'the

St John's First Aid Class c.1910. Front row L–R: R.D. Vaughan, Beach Road; O. Jones, Ty'n Lon; R. Williams, Menai Stores; J.H. Jones, Printer, Bangor Street; W.E. Thomas, Waterloo House (tailor); W.T. Davies, Gwyndre; O.T. Williams, retired manager Dinorwic Quarries; Dr H. Edwards, Instructor, Trefeddyg; Lewis Edwards, slate examiner, Anchor House; T. Francis, tonsorial artist (barber) and taxidermist; R. Williams, Noddfa; J.E. Williams, Noddfa; H.N. Bank, watchmaker, Greenwich House; William Jones, baker, Bangor Street; Griffith Morris, Brynffynon Road; Richard Davies, Quay House. PC Davies is on the extreme left and J. Bank (brother of (H.N. Bank) postman on the extreme right. [Dr Henry Edwards]

First Aid Class 1923. Back row L–R: John G. Jones, W. Francis, W.E. Roberts, Tom B. Owen, Bertie Jones, Edward John Phillips, Owen Jones, PC Jones. Middle row L–R: W. Davies, Dr Hennessey, Tom Francis, D.J. Rowlands. Front row: O.G. Roberts, William Roddick. [W. Wyn Roberts]

Pharmacy, Port Dinorwic', i.e. the Springfield property previously mentioned. One son, Richard, was killed in the First World War whilst another, William John, qualified as a chemist and was employed by Bewell's, Cash Chemists, Pitfield Street, London in 1919 and subsequently at Brynmawr, south Wales. Dr Owen's two spinster daughters remained at the family home.

For some unknown reason, it does not appear that he made any attempt to correct the erroneous impression prevalent in the village of being unqualified and this continued to the day he died as his obituary shows:

> At a Caernarvon hospital the death took place of an old and respected character in Port Dinorwic in the person of Mr Robert Owen, Tan-y-Maes familiarly known as 'Dr Owen'. He was a native of Port Dinorwic being the son of Mr John Owen, who was a well-known farmer and veterinary surgeon. Deceased was over 90 years of age and until lately was about. He had been trained in his early days for the medical profession but did not gain the final certificate in order to qualify as a doctor. Yet his knowledge of medicine and his aptitude for diagnosing cases were well-known in the district and many people went to him for advice and treatment. He possessed a very kind hearted and was always ready to help anyone in trouble. He was always addressed as Dr. [C&DH 19.1.1942]

The bereaved

A bereavement entailed additional expenditure which many could ill-afford. For this reason, it was the custom, described as *danfon* or *offrwm*, when calling to express sympathy with a family's loss, for money to be discreetly passed from hand to hand. Another tangible way of providing assistance, in some rural villages, was for a small table, covered in a white cloth, to be placed outside the front door where sugar, tea, butter or cooked meats could be deposited and used to provide refreshments after the funeral for those who may well have walked many miles to attend.

Up to about 1860 it was the custom at the time of bereavement for the coffin to be carried on the shoulders of four men from the village to Llanfairisgaer cemetery and this continued until one of two horse-drawn hearses, described as the parish hearse and the private hearse, became available. After a service in the house of the bereaved, with a musical director leading the singing, the hearse would leave (with the minister and deacons from the chapel or church directly behind) followed by the family and relatives. More often than not the funerals were very large affairs with the male mourners together behind the relatives and the women following at the rear.

In the 1930s, a horse called Comet, owned by Owen Roberts of the Arvon Tavern, was often to be seen between the shafts of the parish hearse plodding at a respectable pace in due deference to the occasion while his owner perched on high, dressed in his funeral outfit of a long brown coat and a stiff hat, originally black, but, with years of wear, more of a reddish colour. With a horse more used to pulling a coal cart from house to house, Owen Roberts's task with the reins and a whip nearby was not so much to slow *Comet's* pace but more to ensure that the hearse was not overtaken by the mourners. As soon as the service at the cemetery was over, knowing that a feed of hay awaited him, *Comet's* usual drowsy pace was replaced by more of a gallop with the driver clinging to the top of the hearse. [GAS XG/2/144]

6: RELIGION

Llanfairisgaer Church, positioned as it is near to the Menai Strait and two miles outside the village of Felinheli, far outdates any other place of worship built within the village. It is believed to have been built in the thirteenth century but with alterations and additions carried out in later years. A stone set in a wall on the inside of the church and which reads '1644/RDLL' is one indication of such an alteration, while on the outside there is another, inscribed 'Andrew Brereton 1649 Bur House'. The south-facing porch was built in 1865 under the instructions of the renowned architect, Sir Gilbert Scott.

Before the Poor Law of 1834, many of the local parishioners were supported by the church. When necessary, taxes could be levied, as indicated by a parish record entry on 24 April 1776 'agreed to tax of five pence a pound be levied towards defraying ye expence [sic] of making a road to ye church and other necessaries belonging to the parish.'

As far as local worshippers were concerned, the Independent Nonconformist congregation held services in the open air at Aberpwll towards the end of the eighteenth century and later in various houses, including Henfelin, but sermons at these services would be dependent on visiting preachers. Because of the nomadic nature of the services, Thomas Jones of Caeglas decided to open up his house so that regular religious services, prayer meetings and a Sunday school could be held there. His house, known as Capel Caeglas, often had a congregation so large that it overflowed on to the toll road.

Exterior and interior of Llanfairisgaer church. [Len Williams]

Siloh chapel. [Len Williams]

With so much zeal and enthusiasm and a determination to establish a permanent meeting place instead of the hitherto 'kitchen religion', an approach was made to Mr Assheton Smith for a piece of land upon which a chapel could be built. This was granted and Siloh chapel was opened there on 10 March . When the people gathered in Caeglas they received warm refreshments before being led by various chapel dignitaries to Siloh, singing '*Dyma feibl anwyl Iesu*' followed by '*Dyma babell y cyfarfod*' on their arrival at the chapel.

The Wesleyan Methodists living in the Aberpwll area had the choice of either travelling to the nearest chapel or organising their own services. This arrangement continued until a piece of ground was acquired in Siloh in the 1830s where they were able to erect their own chapel at a cost of £200, having had the benefit of local farmers conveying stone from a nearby quarry. Even though the members were generally poor, the debt of £200 incurred in the initial building was quickly cleared.

Siloh chapel Sunday school, c.1940.

The Calvinistic Methodist supporters were similarly limited to visiting Capel Graig (between Felinheli and Penrhosgarnedd), Bethel or Llanrug, all of which were considered to be within walking distance, or conducting their own services locally. Although such travel was inconvenient, nevertheless the Calvinistic Methodist movement was well supported. William Pritchard, Tan-y-Graig, the father of John Pritchard, Rhiwal, not only supported Capel Graig (established in 1814) as a deacon but also walked to worship in Llanrug over a period of fifteen years.

With C. Methodism gaining strength and support such stalwarts as Thomas Roberts, Hendy; William Pritchard, Tan-y-Graig; Mrs Mary Lloyd, Brynadda and others, decided that an approach

be made to buy a piece of land at Siloh to build a chapel. Within twelve months of the acquisition of land, Capel Bethania was built in 1861 at a cost of £282.

At the other hamlet of Tan-y-Maes, services were held at Tanrallt the home of Joseph Thomas, a boat builder and the great grandfather of Rev. Joseph Owen, a Wesleyan minister.

Bethania chapel built in Siloh in 1861.
[Len Williams]

Tŷ Joseph, as it was called in 1819, standing near the Tafarngrisiau toll gate, held very successful services and a Sunday school, indeed the latter was so successful that the overflow was housed in a nearby barn. Since Tanrallt could not be identified with any particular religious order, it was difficult for regular services to be held since a sermon, which would normally be delivered at 2 p.m. or in the evening, would be dependent on itinerant preachers. Fourteen people from the surrounding area of Tafarngrisiau formed the first Tanrallt chapel and met at the house for thirteen years.

Eventually a piece of land between Tan-y-Maes and Tyddyn Perthi, was leased for a period of ninety-nine years at a ground rent of ten shillings per annum. A start was made on the building early in 1832 with seating for 120 people. The building also incorporated a house and stable, all under one roof. It was completed by August of that year at a cost of £162 0s. 4d. Money was either lent free of interest or donated until eventually the debt was cleared.

The congregation at Tan-y-Maes having increased beyond the original estimate, resulted in an extension, together with a new house, being built in 1842 at a cost of £132 1s 10d. Yet another extension was made nine years later, at a cost of £149 8s 7d. By 1865, it was decided that a new chapel should be built on a piece of ground which they successfully acquired in Brynffynnon Road. The building, which could seat 645 worshippers, took two years to build at a cost of £2,400 and was opened on 5 April 1867. Amongst the deacons were W.E. Jones, Glanmenai, who leased the Dinas shipyard, and Richard Cadwaladr Griffith, chemist and postmaster in the village. At the turn of the century, the chapel had 352 members and the Sunday school attracted 285 with an average attendance of 171.

Rev. Morris Hughes (1807–63)

Morris Hughes was born on 11 March 1807 at Fachwen, the son of quarryman Hugh Morris. Having only had the benefit of a basic Sunday-school education, he started work at the quarry at the age of twelve. As the result of a serious injury to his hand, he requested and was granted three months leave of absence from work, a period which he occupied improving his educational standard. He found that his greatest handicap was his inability to either speak or understand English. He eventually overcame this obstacle and received an offer of work on the quay at Port Dinorwic collecting data and recording the number of slates arriving from the quarry and being exported by ship. When Thomas Griffith, the harbour master, died, Morris Hughes was appointed to the post.

Although very involved with his work during a period when the quantity of slate passing through the port was increasing, he still found time to participate in local religious affairs, particularly Sunday schools. As a result he along with Rev. John Huxley (the author's great, great-grandfather) and Rev. D. Jones was appointed with the responsibility for 'the teaching by asking questions' or catechism. With the encouragement of his chapel congregation, he decided to become a minister and was

Rev. Morris Hughes. [GAS]

Elim chapel, Siloh, c.1877. [Len Williams]

appointed in August 1838. He and his wife had fourteen children, but when he died on 21 February 1863, aged 55, there were only eight still alive. He had been preaching for twenty-five years and had lived and worked in Felinheli for approximately thirty-three years.

By 1874, the Wesleyans who worshipped at Siloh realised that the new village was developing away from their community and a decision was taken to build a new chapel in the middle of the new village at a cost of £1,700, with seating for 450 persons so as to allow for an increasing congregation. [GAS VP493] The original harmonium in the new chapel was replaced in October 1910 by a pipe organ and the occasion was celebrated with a recital given by Mr Pritchard of Capel Salem, Caernarfon, with the Rev. Tecwyn Evans officiating. The opportunity was taken at this time to rearrange the stairs leading to the pulpit.

Ministers who officiated at the chapel between 1898 and 1964:

1898–1900	Rev. Nicholas Roberts
1900–05	Rev. Peter Jones Roberts
1905–06	Rev. R.W. Jones
1906–09	Rev. Lewis Owen
1909–12	Rev. D. Tecwyn Evans
1912–13	Rev. Tegla Davies
1913–16	Rev. R.W. Jones
1916–19	Rev. Thomas Hughes
1919–22	Rev. Richard Jones
1922–25	Rev. H. Meirion Davies
1925–28	Rev. R. Conway Pritchard
1928–31	Rev. R.J. Parry
1931–34	Rev. T. Gwilym Roberts
1934–39	Rev. J. Gwyn Jones
1939–45	Rev. R.T. Roberts
1945–49	Rev. R. Vaughan Owen
1949–54	Rev. Gwynfryn Evans
1954–59	Rev. Ifor Jones
1959–64	Rev. John Alun Roberts

According to a letter, dated 21 November 1876, from Thomas Griffith, Wesleyan minister, Elim Chapel in Siloh and two dwelling houses were for sale for £225, but the furniture, pews, lamps, timber floorings, gates, railings and stone pillars would remain the property of the trustees. When sold, the chapel was converted to a house which housed six families.

To cater for the growing community at Dinas, caused by the increasing number of workers at the shipbuilding yard and slate works, a small dwelling house was converted in about 1857 into a Mission Chapel for local residents and visiting sailors.

St Mary's Church. [Len Williams]

The Mission was dependent on peripatetic preachers and, possibly due to the closure of the shipyard only survived until 1902.

St Mary's Church, designed by Weightman and Hadfield of Sheffield, was built directly below Tafarngrisiau Farm, approximately two miles from the ancient parish of Llanfairisgaer church. The foundation stone was laid on 23 September 1864 and the building was consecrated twelve months later. It was extended in 1890 at a cost of £1,000. The vicar, Rev. R.W. Griffith, had been the prime mover in getting the National school established in the village.

Services at St Mary's Church were conducted in Welsh, but the English-speaking families living in the village (including those associated with the Vaynol Estate) were catered for at the Port Church, built in 1863. Port Church, which was never solemnised for marriage, had its twin church in Bethel with a similar design and built in the same period. The services at the Vaynol estate church, for the benefit of the Assheton Smith family and staff, were held each Sunday morning at 11 o'clock immediately after the 10 o'clock service at Port Church, with the officiating clergy conveyed in a horse-

Port Church. [Len Williams]

drawn closed carriage to Vaynol, sometimes accompanied by an organist and one or two vocalists to supplement and possibly enhance the singing. In 1869, services in the chapel were conducted by the Rev. J.M. Maude who was paid £6 for four Sundays.

When the building of Capel Moriah for the Independents was completed in 1862, at a cost of approximately £1,000, rather than close Capel Siloh, it was decided that it would continue to serve the Siloh and Aberpwll communities as there was sufficient support for both congregations. The fact that the incumbent at Capel Moriah, Rev. David Griffith, who lived in Tanrallt, was the son of the minister at Capel Siloh, may have influenced the decision to continue the tie between the two chapels. There were 158 members in the Moriah chapel at the turn of the century while Capel Siloh had 110 members. Moriah had the unusual feature of certain seats being described as

Moriah Chapel orchestra, c.1938. [Bethan Smith]

seti llongwyr (sailor seats), allocated specifically for sailors visiting the port. In about 1930, Moriah chapel in addition to having an organ, also had the benefit of an orchestra made up of local musicians namely: violinists: Vina Davies, Lizzie Jones, Elwyn Edwards, Emyr Jones, Eva Jones, John G. Jones, Goronwy Owen together with clarinettists: R.G. Wilson Roberts, Hugh Owen, Owie Lewis and double bass: Robert Arfon Williams. Other instrumentalists participated from time to time.

Work began on building Bethania chapel in 1912 and, on completion two years later, the old chapel in Siloh was demolished. Bethania also had an orchestra made up of five violins, three clarinets, one flute and with Robert Williams (Llys Myfyr) conducting. The Baptists chose to build their chapel at the bottom of Brynffynnon Road in 1862.

With the growth of teetotalism in the 1830s, Methodism soon made it known that the only way forward was by total abstinence (*dirwest*) rather than temperance (*cymedrol*) which had previously been the rule. Even the pot of ale which formed part of the refreshments provided for itinerant preachers was banned. On the other hand, temperance societies, were formed with the intention of curbing excessive drinking rather than total prohibition and in order to rally people to their cause in the early part of the twentieth century, a Snowdrop

Moriah Chapel Band of Hope, c.1929.

Band was formed which consisted of a group of young girls who gave acting and singing performances.

Religious revivals have occurred periodically since the eighteenth century and that of 1817 had the greatest impact on the Methodist cause. It has been suggested that the revival of the 1830s may have been partly incited by a sermon by John Elias, but, since it coincided with an epidemic of Asiatic cholera which swept through Caernarfonshire, this also may have contributed towards a desire to be 'saved'. The Methodist preachers were Howell Harris, Daniel Rowland, Williams 'Pantycelyn', Thomas Charles, John Jones and the Baptists evangelists were represented by Christmas Evans.

However, it was the revival of 1859 that increased the number of Nonconformists in Wales so that they equalled, if not surpassed, those of the established church. Such an increase caused a change, not only in religious dominance but also in social and possibly political matters. The

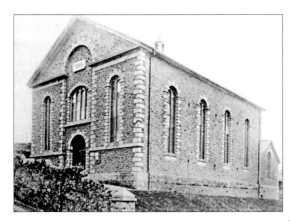

Exterior and interior of Bryn Menai chapel, built in 1864.

various religious movements tried, and no doubt succeeded, to improve the moral standards with their general abhorrence of drink, tobacco and other forms of 'evil'. On the other hand, they may have been responsible for quelling a spirit of enjoyment in the form of old customs or traditions which had prevailed in the countryside. Such was the power of the orators during a *diwigiad* meeting and their ability to arouse feelings that anyone who 'could have contributed towards unbecoming behaviour' would be volubly criticised.

Such was the charisma and reputation of the preachers during these times that people who gathered to listen to their message were ready to be 'saved'. Even those who went to such meetings with the intention of mocking both preacher and congregation would depart deeply humbled and chastened. For anyone without the benefit of such an experience, it is difficult to explain such behaviour. To categorise as mass-hysteria would be an over simplification. The experience seemed to affect all and sundry irrespective of status, social standing or occupation, with everyone swept along determined to repent.

Even between the First and Second World Wars, travelling preachers such as Tom Nefyn and Pastor Jeffreys would call at

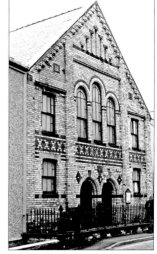

Elim Wesleyan Chapel built in Bangor Street in 1877. [GAS]

Salim Baptist Chapel interior. [Len Williams]

Felinheli to preach in the open air. Other evangelists (or at least persons describing themselves as such) would travel from place to place with a portable harmonium and hold outdoor services called 'Happy on the Way'.

The chapels and churches had governed the lives of most people in Welsh towns and villages over many years but the revival of 1904–05 may well have seen Welsh religion at its zenith. The influence thereafter declined.

Chapels undoubtedly dominated the lives of most people, not only on Sundays but also throughout the week, since most days involved some form of religious devotion, prayer meetings, Bible study classes, choir practices, Band of Hope, literary societies, together with meetings of chapel officials. Directly after the 1904–5 revival and possibly as a consequence of it, members of chapels may well have gone through a period of being subjected to a complete adherence to the Methodist doctrine. Any support

Salim Baptist Chapel deacons, 1930s. [W.Wyn Roberts]

given to an event outside the chapel was generally frowned upon unless it had the blessing of the chapel's minister and deacons. Although enjoyed by many, such support and encouragement did not extend to such pastimes as football, snooker and billiards, which had become popular in the latter part of the nineteenth century. Paradoxically, the Young Men's Christian Association (YMCA) provided amongst other facilities, snooker tables as an inducement to keeping youngsters off the street or out of the pubs.

Bethania Chapel deacons, 1938.
Bethania Sunday school.

Not everyone was unhappy with these 'puritanical attitudes'. Generally speaking, the older the chapel member, the more likely he or she was to accept the strict Methodist doctrine since this was the lifestyle to which they were accustomed. The younger element in society was often resentful at being denied participation and enjoyment in newly-introduced forms of entertainment, especially on a weekday. After the First World War, it was inevitable that demobilised servicemen, having experienced life outside of the villages of Caernarfonshire, possibly for the first time, would have a different outlook when they returned home.

The sanctity of Sundays declined after the Second World War but, despite this, public houses in Port Dinorwic remained shut on Sundays and places of worship continued to

Local chapel pageant 1920s (photograph taken in the Arvonia yard).

Snowdrop Band 1880.

draw support. The prominent sign on the wall of the local barber which read 'God is the head of this house; the unseen guest at every meal; the silent listener to every conversation' was further proof if such was required, of the atmosphere in the village at that time. There was a certain stigma attached to those who were not members of a church or chapel, and all members of the community were encouraged to participate in activities of one religious denomination or another. Perhaps regular attendance was regarded as a form of insurance for the 'after life'.

From a village which supported six chapels and two churches, Felinheli now (2013) has only one church and one chapel. Many of the old chapels and churches built in the nineteenth and early twentieth centuries with the sacrificial halfpennies and pennies of the poor, have closed and either been demolished or converted to some other use. Some denominations, not quite so pedantic as in olden days, have combined under one roof to form an united congregation.

Urdd yr Eirlys. [Bethan Smith]

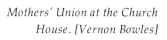

Mothers' Union at the Church House. [Vernon Bowles]

7. EDUCATION

The population of Llanfairisgaer for 1811 is given as 275 (British Parliamentary Papers – Education Poor Classes, Session 1819) and no schools are recorded in the parish. It stated 'the poor classes send their children for education to the neighbouring parishes of Bangor and Carnarvon, where they are amply provided with the means in schools supported by charitable contributions'. The report went on to say that with a population of 66,448 in Caernarfonshire, there were 3,766 children under daily instruction and 23,223 in Sunday Schools, adding that, as an inducement to improve attendance, a certain charity in Bangor gave £2 in order to clothe 'the poor children who attend school'.

Until official state-funded education became available, schools in Felinheli were limited to those run privately or as Sunday schools although it appears that a day school, run by Moses Parry of Pant-yr-Afallen, existed in Vaynol in 1777. Other accounts state that a similar school run by Rev. Hugh Jones from Liverpool was available at Capel Graig, but it is doubtful if many children from the hamlet of Aberpwll would have undertaken the two-mile or so journey to Capel Graig when a so-called private school was available in Siloh. Education was not a high priority amongst people who spent the greater part of their working lives in the quarry, in agriculture or in domestic service.

Some two miles along the toll road in the direction of Caernarfon, a Calvinistic Methodist Chapel established in Tan-y-Maes in 1819, had 110 scholars being taught in Sunday school in the 1820s.

A private school, established in 1828 at Tanrallt (known as Tŷ Joseph) near Tafarngrisiau, was run by a young lady from Glangwna, Caeathro. When she married William Hughes, a teacher at Capel Graig, they went to live in Amlwch. When they returned to Felinheli in about 1850 they lived at Helen Cottage where they ran a school called by some *Ysgol Bwt*. The pupils who attended this school were described as being 'from the respectable families of the village' and 'the education that they received enabled them to fill the roles of preachers and foremen in the commercial or maritime world. Although small, schools such as *Ysgol Bwt* at least gave pupils a basic educational grounding and direction. The education returns for 1833, (which ggave the population of Llanfairisgaer as 379) showed that the only education available was through the Established Church Sunday School where 'gratuitous teachers give tuition to 10 males and 15 females'.

Perhaps the best known private school in Felinheli was that run by Thomas Griffith (1781–1861) who charged each child one penny per week. It was established in a room at the back of Elim Chapel before moving to the property known as Clwb Siloh during the 1840s. His purported academic knowledge was off-set by his style of teaching which was described as 'clumsy and lacked planning' simply because he had not had the benefit of teacher training. Nevertheless, it did at least introduce children to school discipline and provided them with some education which would be of benefit in later life. Apart from a short period away in Llanrug and Bethel during 1843–5 when the Rev. Hugh Roberts from Bangor taught at Siloh, Griffith continued in the role of a teacher for many years. He reputedly seldom, if ever, referred to the children's given name but rather as 'you Halfway lad', or 'Robin Hughes's lad' or 'Sion Pritchard's boy'. When he was in a good mood, which was, apparently, very seldom, he wasted time describing such matters as ghosts and spirits resulting in the children being even more frightened of him. He was however very fond of birds especially 'night birds' and on one occasion, he brought an owl from the Vaynol woods to the school. Griffith enjoyed being invited to tea at a pupil's house and to gain his favour children often sought permission from their mother for such an invitation to be made. Individuals from the village who had experienced attending the school were Rev. Thomas Gwynedd Roberts; Thomas Hughes (Bodarborth); David Evans (Dinorwic House); Thomas Jones (Anwylfa) and John Pritchard (Belmont).

An account written in 1893 by Bob, Ty'n Brwynog, Earlestown, Lancashire, described his mother's experience some sixty years previously of attending the so-called school at Siloh:

It was housed initially in a room at the rear of the Wesleyan chapel which consisted of a floor partly of wood and the remainder of soil. The two small windows admitted a little light and an abundance of 'fresh air' came through the doorway. About three dozen children attended

Council School c.1908.

Council School c.1910. Mary, Dr Owen's daughter, a pupil teacher, is standing on the right of the back row.

Aberpwll school opening 1927.

the school and the master, Thomas Griffith, was described by the writer as being very large. He had a spectacle and, due to a bad limp, walked with a stick. He wore a large beaver hat and a suit that never varied. Due to its age and condition it was difficult to describe its original colour especially the jacket with its 'swallow tail'. Griffith was described as a cruel person who maintained discipline by means of a ruler and birch rod which he applied regularly and effectively especially if he heard Welsh being spoken. It resulted in the children being so constantly terrified of these instruments of torture that the act of learning became of secondary importance.

The writer continued 'when Thomas Griffith's time came to an end as a schoolmaster he was put under the care of the Fodol Isa family and it was there that I (Bob) had the opportunity of getting to know him personally'. When he died he was buried in Llanfairisgaer cemetery and a 'noble gravestone was erected by his past scholars to mark his grave'.

Other altruistic individuals who provided village children with some basic knowledge included Miss Williams who lived at Glanrafon Cottage until about 1874 and Miss Pritchard at Y Glyn, a farmhouse at Aberpwll. Other private schools were established in different parts of the village, including one at 2 Port Terrace run by a Miss Davies. Tuition was also provided at an orphanage established in the Cocoa Rooms in Bangor Street by Mrs Wynn Griffith of Llanfair Hall.

On 16 April 1845, 'John Griffith Griffith of Llanfair Hall conveyed to the Bishop of Bangor and his successors a piece of land near to Tafarnygrisiau in the parish of Llanfairisgaer for the purpose of building a school thereon for the poor children of the parish also a house for the schoolmaster'.

No doubt influenced by such a gift Thomas Assheton Smith subscribed £30 towards the expense of erecting what was to be the National School which opened later that year. [GAS VP7160]

The National School, which was open to government inspectors, had as its governors, the curates and other administrators of the parish, together with three other persons belonging to the Church of England and living within seven miles of the parish church of Llanfairisgaer. This was the only licensed elementary school in the village for many years. The 1847 'Blue Book' report on the school stated:

> In Llanfairisgaer (National School) the master was formerly a shopkeeper. Having been disabled by an accident from active work, he became a schoolmaster and spent two months and a half at Carnarvon to learn the National System. He speaks very broken English both in points of grammar and pronunciation; and his questions on Scripture are feeble.

The only favourable comment made in the report concerning the Llanfairisgaer National School was 'The building is handsome and well finished with fixtures and other necessary apparatus' but went on to say 'The greater part of the Master's income is derived from the childrens' pence'.

In an attempt at improving the standard of teaching, a department was formed in the National School in Caernarfon in 1846 with a view to training masters for Church schools but 'the master was himself trained for three weeks only more than ten years ago'. This was to develop into the Normal College (now part of Bangor University).

The infamous 1847 'Blue Book' report on education emphasised the prominence that was to be given to language teaching and stated that the 'professed object for which day schools have been established in North Wales is to teach the English language'. In Caernarfonshire one school gave instructions in Welsh out of 591 schools (the only one in the then six counties of north Wales) while seventy-one taught through the medium of English and a further seven in both languages. Although Welsh was the language of the home and of play, from the turn of the century all subjects in the local schools were taught through the medium of English. The teachers were,

W.L. Roberts and the pupils of Llanfairisgaer National School at Vaynol c.1918.

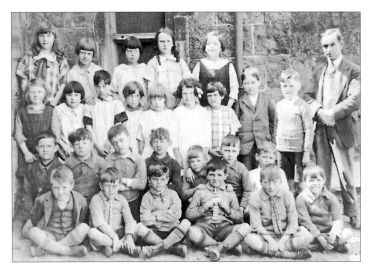

Llanfairisgaer National School with D.J. Rowlands (headmaster) c.1920. [Len Williams] Top row: Nancy Allman; Beatrice Owen; Katie Jones; Lily B. Evans; Mary Roberts. 2nd row: Doris Smith; Nancy Elias; Nellie Owen; Beti Owen; Nancy Hope; Rosie Bradley; Ruth Hughes; Roby Williams; Owen Parry. 3rd row: Tommy Chambers; Ifor (Dinas); Bob Owen; John Parry; Harry Chubb; William Pierce; Gwilym Davies. 4th row: John Owen; Hugh Pierce Jones; John (Brynwaen); Emlyn Parry; Owen Emrys Hughes; John Llewelyn Jones.

however, fully competent in both languages and individuals who experienced schooling during this period expressed the opinion that they were not in any way the worse for the method of teaching as it gave them a good grounding in both languages. By 1912, a report on Llanfairisgaer school recorded that it was 'an exceedingly well conducted school' and that 'an excellent spirit of work is shown by the children. The fact that the children were able to answer questions through the medium of Welsh and English clearly indicates that instruction was given in both languages'. The head at this time was Mr David Jones (1906-19), assisted by six teachers.

The Llanfairisgaer National School was extended in 1872 but, within three years, a report on the structure of the school stated:

> … found the cracks [in the walls to be] … very old and there are no signs of any danger, drainage system is in a very unsatisfactory state, the drains being choked up through deficiency of water.

Llanfairisgaer National School 1930 with D.J. Rowlands (headmaster).

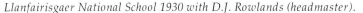

Aberpwll School, c.1935. [Nesta Easton] L-R: Back row: Mair Roberts; Mona Thomas; Vera Roderick; Olive Gardner; Doreen Jones; Ella Carr. Second row: Nesta Pierce; Helen Jones, Albert Jones; Arfon Roberts; Robert Smith; Roy Nicholas, Frederick Branchett; Sylvia Williams; Jean Allman. Third row: Mara Jones; Megan Jones; Jeannie Roderick, Megan Williams; Mona Pritchard; Nancy Williams. Front row: Emyr Jones; Robert Arthur Williams; Meirion Jones; Arwyn Owen; Evie Robert; Hubert Jones.

The roof requires pointing the whole of the timber work requires painting both inside and outside. The school fixtures are rather dilapidated and old. The Privies for the children are in a very bad state and not fit: they should be attended to immediately. [GAS VP2956]

Despite these shortcomings the school was described as being very successful in that it gained grants over the years to assist in its teaching and by 1903 the sum of £110 went towards teaching 180 children.

Since education at this school at that time was limited to children who attended the Church of England, the Rev. David Griffith, minister of Moriah Chapel, undertook the task of establishing a day school in a room beneath Moriah Chapel in 1868 with an education based on the Puritan schools. This was the only Nonconformist school in the village for five years and was 'of great benefit to the area in general'. It did, however, have two major problems: funds were low and the room being used was considered dark and unhealthy for the children. The teaching however, was so successful that when an application was made for a grant, this was allowed on condition the school moved to better premises. After futile attempts to find alternative accommodation, the government inspector condemned the room and refused to allow any further grants. The 120 to 140 children who attended the school had to be shared out between the Bethel school and the

Council School 1938. [Mona Thomas] Back row: T. Arfon Roberts; Reg Chambers Jones; John Pierce Jones; Albert Jones; Owen –?– (Fron Deg). Second row: Dilys Morgan; Margaret Williams; Vona Williams; Mona Thomas; Margaret Williams; Maisie Owen; Menai Jones; Mara Jones. Third row: Selwyn Williams; Eileen Jones; Joan Pennington; Buddyg Hughes; Gwilym Jones. Fourth row: Emyr Jones; Cyrus Hughes; John Edward Williams; –?–; Evan Hugh Jones; Berwyn Williams.

National school and it was not until 17 November 1874 that a successful request was made for land on which to build new premises. Plans were then drawn up and a committee formed under the chairmanship of the Rev. Thomas Griffith minister at Elim Chapel.

The British Board School's (confusingly known initially as the British School, the Board School, the Britannia School, the Council School and, in later years, Ysgol Newydd (the new school) log book for 1876–91 provides us with some insight into the day-to-day activities of the school. When it was opened by Mr T.J. Williams from Bangor Normal College on 1 December 1876 it had 127 pupils on the register. Within a week, the number of pupils had risen to 171 and continued to rise until the end of the following year when the figure reached 250. The building, located at the top of Brynffynnon Road, measured twenty yards by eight yards and cost £455 12s 6d but, with fittings and furniture, the total came to £526 3s 8d. Voluntary contributions towards this sum amounted to £276 3s 8d and a further £50 was received on the opening day, leaving a deficiency of £200 which was shared amongst the six chapels in the village with each deciding how they would raise the necessary funds.

An entry made on 21 December 1876 stated: 'The disorder and want of discipline in school is disheartening. Children have no idea of order. Reform must be gradual. [GAS XES1/103/1] The school staff in 1878 was listed as T.J. Williams (Headmaster), H.T. Ellis (assistant master); Miss Evans (serving mistress) and four monitors. A note made on the 3 May 1878 stated: 'The boundary wall of the school having been built, we have made a rule to the effect that 'no Welsh is to be spoken within the school ground. We find it difficult to enforce the rule'.

Although schools had to abide within strict rules and regulations, discipline within the schools had not improved greatly as shown in a note made at the Council school on 6 September 1878 'on Friday I had to punish fifteen of the children for being absent the previous day gathering blackberries and have also a number absenting themselves for the purpose of fetching milk'.

Inevitably, with the villagers having connections with the sea, the loss of a vessel could have repercussions on local families. This happened on 28 October 1892 with the loss of the schooner

Aberpwll School c.1944. As the result of kitchen facilities being installed in the school, the children were able to partake of a mid-day meal for the first time. The event must have been regarded as important for the school governors to be present as well as the two teachers, Miss Griffith (from Bethesda) and Miss Griffith (from Bethel). [Arnold Hughes]

Annie and six lives. The register made the observation 'The loss cast a gloom on the whole of the neighbourhood. Many local families and pupils affected'. [GAS XES/103/2]

The school diary noted on 22 June 1897, Queen Victoria Diamond Jubilee Day: 'In the afternoon the children marched to Llanfair Hall where a treat had been kindly provided by Capt. Wynn Griffith for the schools of Port Dinorwic (Board and National) Bethel (Board) and Llanddeiniolen (National)'.

The *Caernarfon and Denbigh Herald* for 21 January 1898 reported that W.R. Davies, who had been headmaster at the Council School between *c*.1887 and 1898, was leaving to work in Swansea and a presentation was made to him by R.C. Griffith, Medical Hall, the Chairman of the School Board, with William Lloyd Roberts (1853–1908), headmaster of the National School in attendance. [GAS XM4662/2, XS1243/18] Davies was succeeded by S. Currie who continued as headmaster for thirty-five years, retiring on 27 July 1932.

As the result of the closure of the Mission Church in Dinas, a note was made in the register on 17 March 1902 that the [Council] School had 'Received a present of a harmonium from the Mission Church'.

Even in May 1904 absenteeism continued to be a problem for various reasons including (according to the school register) children visiting the 'Buffalo Bill' show in Caernarfon. As a result, an attendance officer named Mr Ayres was employed to rectify the situation. His job was later undertaken by Paul Roberts, a farmer from Caeathro, who was known to everyone as Sergeant Paul. He would call at the home of every child that was absent from a school to establish the reason and, unless a reasonable explanation was forthcoming, the culprit and possibly the parent were admonished with the child being promptly escorted to school. On occasions, the reason given was that the child did not possess a pair of shoes or boots to wear for school, or that the only pair was being repaired. Without a great deal of sympathy or compassion, the parents were asked why they had not applied for parish relief.

As a means of alleviating problems within a family, and in particular as a means of reducing absenteeism, a clothing club was established in 1891 whereby wealthy persons such as the Assheton Smiths contributed sums of money which were distributed to the needy. A note made on 7 November 1891 stated that 'a bonus of £5 given by G.W.D. Assheton Smith to the Clothing Club was distributed today in sums ranging from 1s 6d to 3s 7d according to the number of attendances made by the children'. The log book noted on Tuesday, 22 February 1898 that 'Mr Ayres attendance officer visited the school, very heavy list of absentees to call upon'. [GAS XES/73/1] A further note made 1 March 1939 stated that 'Provision of footwear and clothing for certain children by the unemployment Assistance Board or Public Assistance Committee had been made'.

Since there was a dearth of entertainment for village children, a change in the routine was always welcomed by the pupils, especially when it entailed finishing school early as was the case on 2 June 1904 'to attend Bostock's and Wombwell's Menagerie Nature Study'.

The latter part of the nineteenth century was a period when children were able to play in safety along the main street. The only traffic that was liable to 'stop play' was the occasional horse-drawn type. This scenario continued until the early cars appeared. Later, youngsters had their own paddling pool and a playground on Beach Road which was looked after by Robert Roberts who conveniently lived in a nearby houseboat. Since he was responsible for closing the play area at sunset he was inevitably known to everyone as 'Robbie Sunset'.

The 1908 *Carnarvonshire Education Committee Handbook* stated that Llanfairisgaer Church of England School, with David Jones as headmaster, had certified accommodation for 141 boys and girls and 90 infants making a total of 231. At this time however, there were only 193 children on the books, with an average attendance of 147. By comparison, the Council School, with Mr S. Currie as headmaster, had certified accommodation for 150 boys and girls and a further 100 in the infants section making a total of 250, but with 257 children on the books and an average attendance of 217. Only two years earlier, a writer outlined the great improvements which had taken place in the education of the children:

Velinheli has made great strides as far as education is concerned especially when a comparison is made between the education available 40–50 years ago (*c*.1850) in Tanrallt and Siloh. Without being critical of the old teachers in the early schools, there has been a great improvement in the level of education. The teaching was both ineffective and incomplete when compared with present teaching. Today we have good buildings which are airy and healthy and of benefit to studious children. Discipline has improved as have standards in teaching and knowledge. There is interest and a greater desire to learn with a realisation that it is a privilege I believe that there is no one unmindful of that which the old teachers accomplished in poor buildings which were dark, small and unhealthy and, consequently, had a deep respect for them [sic]. They, in fact, laid the foundation for present day education without having had the education, facilities or qualification for such a task. Nevertheless, the pupils grew up to be responsible people that were of tremendous service to the district.

A report published in 1911 by the Organisation of Education in Carnarvonshire stated:

Llanfairisgaer National School, 1948, with D.J. Rowlands (headmaster – left) and Owen Williams. [Derek Roberts]

The committee have rightly taken the view that their duty is to secure the material conditions of educational success by providing adequate accommodation everywhere so that no child may have unreasonable distance to walk to school and that every child when in school may have plenty of space, pure air and fresh water … Continuation classes provided: Council School – Practical Arithmetic 23 attended, Welsh 23 attended, needlework 20 attended, singing 64 attended'.

The HMI report of 28 September 1912 stated that new desks were to be provided without delay at Llanfairisgaer School but went on to say:

This is an exceedingly well conducted school (and) an excellent spirit of work is shown by the children. They answer readily when questioned in Welsh as well as in English. This may be accounted for by the fact that they are given much conversational practice in both languages in all their lessons. David Jones, the headmaster, at this time had six teachers with him at the school.

Various evening classes were available in 1912 including an 'ambulance class'. However, the report stated that by 1919 needlework and English classes had fallen through because of lack of support. Practical arithmetic thirty five attended, mensuration thirty five attended, mechanics and drawing thirty five attended, needlework, domestic economy and literature nineteen attended. [GAS EA1, ES1]

In 1912, when most householders grew their own vegetables, gardening formed part of the Council School curriculum with vegetable seeds being obtained from O.R. Williams, Drug and Grocery Stores on Bangor Street.

The 1913 returns of the Council School stated that the headmaster, Mr S. Currie received a salary of £150 per annum while the twenty-eight year old Mary Owen (1885–1947) (of the Pharmacy, Port Dinorwic), a supplementary teacher, only received a salary of £30 per annum (a note made in the school diary on 2 July 1936 stated that: 'Mrs Mary Jones (née Owen, 1885–1947, the daughter of Dr Robert Owen, a member of the school committee) who was on the staff of this school 13 years ago as a pupil teacher and assistant mistress and who emigrated to Oakland, California, paid a visit to school today and gave interesting details of American schools in the states where she resides and works as a teacher.'

Conditions in local schools generally were often very difficult. During the 1920 coal strike for instance, the stock of coal at the National School was exhausted early in the year and it was necessary to burn old pieces of railing rather than see the children suffering from the cold. Even when authority was given to buy coal locally, or borrow from the Council School, the situation was further exacerbated when their meagre supply was stolen from the coal shed during the Christmas vacation.

There were always close links between the local schools and the Vaynol family and, in the period after the First World War, young children were marched from the Council School to Vaynol at Christmas time. They would sing as they passed through the village and continued doing so until they reached Vaynol where a tea party and a gift from Lady Assheton Smith awaited them. They were also given an apple and a bun for their walk home. Sir Michael Duff continued with this tradition but with the tea party taking place in the Memorial Hall rather than in Vaynol with the catering carried out by Misses Thomas from the Temperance Café.

The increasing population in the Aberpwll area led parents to campaign for a new infants school to be built to avoid very young children having to walk some two miles to the National or Council school at the other end of the village. Despite this appeal, and a revolt amongst the parents who kept their children away from school in December 1912, it took until 28 November 1927 before a school described as the Aberpwll Infant School was opened with twenty eight children and Miss G.M. Griffith as Head Teacher and Miss Ellen Thomas as an uncertificated assistant. [GAS ES/1]

D.J. Rowlands 'took charge of the National school' on 17 March 1919 with an annual salary of £338 6s 8d and two months later, a presentation was made to his predecessor, Mr David Jones, who had been headmaster for twelve years, by Mrs Wynn Griffith. Mr Rowlands, who retired

Aberpwll school 1956.
[Charlotte Evans]
Back L-R: Keith Crosby; Maldwyn Hughes; Barry Jones; Eifion Jones: Richard Hughes.
Middle: Austin Jones; Maureen Bradnock; Pat O'Shaughnessy; Megan Pritchard; Catherine Williams; Eluned Jones; Meirion Jones;
Front: Andrew Cunnah; Carys Jones; Charlotte Williams; Irene Roberts; Gillian Ellis; Philip –?–.

on 25 March 1949 having attained the age of sixty-five, was considered by many to have been both an excellent teacher and headmaster.

An entry in the school log book dated July 1951 recorded 'This afternoon the school will be closing its doors for the last time after serving the village of Port Dinorwic for 106 years'. [GAS XES/73/3]

Between the two wars, discipline in the schools was strict and many recall the fear that was created by the sound of the school bell, particularly if they were late. The thought of seeing David Jones, the headmaster, standing outside the school to catch the latecomers, struck terror into many a young heart. Not surprisingly, there were many pupils and ex-pupils alike who were delighted to see the school bell permanently silenced when the old school finally closed in 1949 to be replaced by a modern building, which catered for all children, irrespective of denomination or creed.

8: Transport

The first turnpike trust to be introduced in north Wales was in Denbighshire and Flintshire, and included the road between Tal-y-Cafn ferry and Conwy. The road between Bangor ferry and Holyhead, which passed through Penymynydd and Llangefni, came under the control of the Anglesey Trust which was set up in 1765. When the Caernarvonshire Turnpike Trust became operational four years later, the first section of the toll road which it became responsible for began in Conwy and proceeded through Bangor, Bangor ferry and Caernarfon as far as Pwllheli.

Each trust was given statutory powers, usually over a term of twenty-one years, to maintain certain sections of road to an approved standard and to levy tolls on travellers passing over them. Turnpikes were let annually, either by tender or auction, and were advertised in local papers. Although the keepers responsible for collecting the tolls had the benefit of a tollhouse, they had an onerous task since they had to be on duty day and night each and every day of the year and they inevitably had to bear the resentment of travellers who were very much against the principle of tolls.

Within the parish of Llanfairisgaer in 1792, individuals who were involved in statutory road maintenance by providing wagons for transporting materials were: John Rowlands, Crûg; Williams Price, Plas Brereton; Robert Williams, Parkia; Thomas Morris, Bryn; William Jones, Tan-y-Maes; Morris Williams, Bodandreg. Others named were William Humphreys and John Edwards, Bush Farm; William Rowlands, Tynperthi; Evan Williams, Prysgol; Thomas Williams, Penrallt and Grace Griffiths, Garddfon Inn. [UWB Porth-yr-Aur 3426]

The old road from Bangor to Aberpwll and Caernarfon, which had been in existence for many years, was improved with the establishment of the Caernarvonshire Turnpike Trust in 1769 and the building of the turnpike road in 1776. From Bangor it passed through Penchwintan, Penrhos-garnedd, Capel Graig and then over land which was subsequently incorporated within the Vaynol estate wall. As they approached Aberpwll, travellers encountered the first tollhouse which may well have been the property now

Turnpike on Caernarfon Road (right).
Note the street light and telephone wires
sharing the same pole. [John Hughes]

known as the smithy, since no other building is shown on contemporary Vaynol estate maps. The toll road then continued through Aberpwll, past the Halfway House Inn, to the second turnpike at Tafarngrisiau, before continuing across country to Cerrig-yr-Afon and on to Caernarfon.

Anyone refusing to pay tolls was liable to have any animal, goods or chattels seized and these would be sold within five days with the difference repaid to the owner if the toll remained unpaid. Public stage-coaches had to pay tolls on return journeys within the same day. Various people were allowed to travel toll free, such as clergy going to visit the sick, a funeral being held in another parish, or officers and soldiers who were carrying materials to reopen roads or bridges.

With the arrival of the railways and the resulting loss of revenue suffered by the Turnpike Trust, the Local Government Act of 1888 resulted in county councils and county borough councils becoming responsible for main roads. The Caernarvon Turnpike Trust came to an end with an announcement in the *North Wales Chronicle* on 4 November 1882 which stated that the 'removal of the bars and turnpike gates is now being proceeded with. Travellers thereafter are able to travel along trust roads without being charged a toll'. [GAS QR/TT/14, QR/TT/15, QR/TT/21, QR/TT/addt 4]

London & North Western Railway

When the Chester to Holyhead line was completed, a single branch line was built (by the contractors, McCormick and Holmes) from Menai Bridge initially to Felinheli where the first train arrived in March 1852. To enable the construction of a further single line to Caernarfon, discussions took place between the railway company and Lord Boston, as to whether the railway which needed to cross the turnpike road, a half-a-mile or so from the station, should do so by means of a bridge or a railway-crossing. Although traffic was limited to an occasional horse and cart or trap, the decision was taken that a bridge would be less disruptive, particularly to the railway. A bridge would also enable the toll road to be diverted so as to pass beneath the bridge rather than continuing through Augusta Street, as had been the case for many years. Once free of traffic, Augusta Street was renamed Augusta Place, and the railway bridge became known as

Railway crossing on the road leading to Dinas and Beach Road. [Emyr Owen]

Class 4 2-6-4 Tank engine (Nᵒ· 80094) heading a train from Bangor to Afonwen, 1957. [Len Williams]

Pont Tafarn-y-Bush or Pont-y-Taproom (this latter being a reference to a small cottage on Augusta Street established by 1832 by the Garddfon Inn as a convenient place for toll road travellers to partake of refreshments).

The official opening of the Bangor to Caernarfon railway took place on 1 July 1852, when a special train left Liverpool arriving in Caernarfon at 11 a.m. The occasion was marked with a 'salute of 20 guns being fired from a spot opposite the station and sustained by a similar salute from Porth yr Aur battery'. The passengers on board, including the superintendent of the line, were then taken to the George Hotel at Menai Bridge where 'they were entertained to a banquet by the railway contractors at 3 p.m'.

With the arrival of the railway, Thomas Assheton Smith took the opportunity to present a plan to divert the lower part of the 1812 Nant-y-Garth road. Instead of it passing through Siloh and down to the wharf-side as before, its direction would be altered to connect directly with the nearby toll road. This was approved and proceeded with. [GAS X/RD/12/1851]

The Griffiths family of Plas Llanfair who owned land between Felinheli and Caernarfon, was also affected by the railway passing over its property. Possibly as an appeasement, a halt was built in 1854 by the railway contractors close to their home. The halt was thereafter referred to as Griffith's Crossing (John Ridgway was appointed station master at the halt in 1871).

The passenger service between Bangor and Caernarfon initially consisted of four

Goods train at Port Dinorwic station.
[Len Williams]

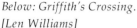

Griffith's crossing c.1967.
E. Norman Kneale.

Below: Griffith's Crossing.
[Len Williams]

weekday trains each way, and two on Sundays, but due to increasing patronage, this was increased by the 1860s to six trains on weekdays and three on Sundays. By 1867, the Bangor & Caernarfon Railway had been taken over by the London & North Western Railway Company.

Within four years, the decision was taken to double the line between Bangor and Caernarvon and to replace the original station that was located behind the Halfway House Inn with a new and larger station nearer to the developing village at a cost of £2,980. The new station would have a general waiting room, a ladies waiting room, a station master's office, a booking office, toilets and an oil lamp room. Facilities at the station included the means to load and unload animals from trucks as well as other cargo. The first stationmaster, named Isaac Jones, and his successors, lived in a flat above the station building.

The arrival of the railway provided new and more convenient means of travel and introduced passengers to the pleasures of seaside resorts along the coast. During the twentieth century, the railway also provided football excursions for enthusiasts to see Liverpool, Everton and other teams playing at the cost of a 5s return ticket.

Port Dinorwic Station staff c.1920. The person seated on the left is Joseph Edwin Jones a noted local singer. [Len Williams]

A motor car parked near Miss Morris's shop (opposite the Council School on Brynffynnon Road), 1920s.
[W. Wyn Roberts]

Early motor cars

The introduction of the motor car at the beginning of the twentieth century provided individuals, who could afford such a luxury, an alternative way of travelling. Some of the earliest cars registered in Port Dinorwic were:

CC75 De-Dion 3hp, registered 19 July 1904. Owner: Ernest Jones, Bodarborth, Port Dinorwic.
CC121 Progress 3 4$\frac{1}{2}$hp (black and yellow), long chassis. Owner: Reginald Paxton Harding, Bryntirion, Vaynol, 17 May 1905.
CC136 Daimler motor wagon (varnished oak), 4 November 1905. Owner: Charles Gardner Assheton Smith, Vaynol Park.
CC138 (green and black). Owner: Reginald Paxton Harding, Bryntirion, Vaynol.
CC167 De-Dion 4hp, (dark blue with white line), 19 May 1906. Owner: Arthur William Arthurton, Bryn Adda, Vaynol.

CC170 Rover 6hp two-seater (body black with white line). Owner: Robert Pierce, Bod Meirion Port Dinorwic.
CC186 Daimler 28/36hp Daimler, (black body, natural wood varnished, chassis painted yellow), shooting brake, 11 September 1906. Owner: Vaynol.
CC316 16hp, 20 August 1909 (dark blue). Owner:

Robert Pierce (Bod Meirion) and John Edward Williams in a 1906 6hp Rover car. [W. Wyn Roberts]

William Lloyd Williams, Bodarwy, Port Dinorwic.

CC448 Napier 30hp (dark blue), 17 June 1911. Owner: Ernest Albert Neale, Plas Dinorwic, Port Dinorwic.

CC496 20hp (black), 18 November 1911. Owner: William Lloyd Williams, Bodarwy, Port Dinorwic.

CC599 Léon Bollée 20/30hp, limousine (dark green), 20 May 1913. Owner: F. Richmond Brown, Llanfair Hall, Port Dinorwic.

CC554 Renault 20/30hp, landaulette (yellow and black), 2 November 1912, (owner not given).

Mrs Anne Owen, daughter of Robert Owen, postmaster, April 1935. [Kathleen W. Roberts]

CC1007 Ford 20hp, 5-seater, 8 May 1914. Owner: R.W. Owen, Halfway Inn, Port Dinorwic.

CC1016 Studebaker Flanders 15hp, 9 May 1914. Owner: Thomas Owen, 36 Bangor Street, Port Dinorwic.

CC1140 Ford Model T (black), 2 October 1914, 4-seater, tourer. Owner: Dr Henry Edwards, Trefeddyg, Port Dinorwic.

CC2456 Ford 20hp (blue), 3 August 1920. Owner: Robert Williams, Eiffel Café, Port Dinorwic.

The village had four petrol outlets in the 1920s: Central Garage, selling one grade of Shell at 11d per gallon; Arfon Garage on the Caernarfon Road; Arvonia shop, which sold it in cans with a brass screw-top sealed to confirm the quantity, and, in the 1930s, petrol known as Russian Oil Products, or ROP, was available at a competitive price at the railway station where it was dispensed from a railway tanker in a nearby siding.

Bus Services

Until purpose-built vehicles became available, the first buses to appear on the roads of Anglesey and Caernarfonshire took the form of motor lorries with wooden seats being provided for passengers. Early buses had initials such as INU and UNU (abbreviations for 'I Need You' and 'You Need Us'), inscribed on the side of the bus.

Robert John Roberts ran a Ford bus between Bangor and Caernarfon circa 1920 accompanied by his fourteen year old sister, May, who acted as conductor. Passengers, having boarded the vehicle through a rear door with heads kept low to avoid the roof, sat seven on each side facing each other on wooden seats. Roberts had a workshop at Hafod-yr-Haf, between Bangor and Port Dinorwic, where any faults could be rectified. The Llanfairisgaer Parish Council minutes recorded in November 1927 that the UNU motors were by this time running a service from Port Dinorwic to Caernarfon via Bethel. Other small bus companies such as Bangor Blue, Caernarfon

UNU (You Need Us) bus.

Bangor Blue Motors 1921 with owner and drive. [GAS]

Red, Llandudno Silver, Cynfi Motors, Seiont Motors and Peris Motors operated between various villages and towns. As a result of the Crosville Moor Services purchasing Richards' Busy Bee Service (which consisted of six vehicles and a garage in Crown Street in 1925), the company was able to operate between Caernarfon and Porthmadog, Pwllheli, Llanberis and Dinorwic. The UNU company, including a small garage in South Penrallt, was purchased by Crosville in 1930.

Crosville Motor Services, established in the Chester area in 1911, had by the 1930s taken over most of the small bus companies in Anglesey and Caernarfonshire and, as a result their field of operation had extended to cover most of north and mid Wales.

When war was declared in 1939, Crosville had to be prepared to provide a service at short notice to the numerous army camps and airfields, the Air Ministry at Glyn Peris and NECACO (aircraft factory) at Llanberis. The latter required twenty-three buses, twice a day, to carry employees for both day and night shifts. This was in addition to all the other contractors that required transport as well as covering the needs of the public. The fact that many of the drivers and conductors had been called up to the forces exacerbated the situation even further and many male conductors were replaced by women. During the war, for those who had spent an evening in Caernarfon, the last public service bus to outlying villages, departed from Caernarfon at 10 p.m. but this depended on the availability of a

Royal Blue bus c.1930.

vehicle. If buses were required urgently elsewhere, they were taken off normal service at short notice leaving the public without transport. This shortage resulted in seats being rearranged along both sides of the vehicle to allow plenty of standing room. As the result of the blackout, no lights were allowed inside the vehicles at night and the light emanating from the masked headlamps made driving very hazardous.

Local ladies preparing for an outing with Whiteway buses. [Len Williams]

9: LEISURE

Village Hall

Until a purpose-built village hall became available, indoor entertainment was restricted to events such as the annual eisteddfod which were appropriate for chapels to stage. In 1908, Charles Assheton Smith agreed to donate a site for a village hall and to provide the slates for its roof, on condition that sufficient money was available to cover all other costs and that nothing would be set against local rates. Possibly due to lack of funds, no further progress was made at that time.

The fact that the village lacked a public hall where concerts and other events could be held was mentioned at a meeting of the Llanfairisgaer Parish Council in March 1916 and in particular 'that steps should be taken to obtain land for building a Public Hall'.

Soon after the First World War ended, an army hut was purchased for £100 from Kinmel Camp near Bodelwyddan and was erected near to where the eventual Memorial Hall was built. This enabled additional functions to be held in the village.

Conservative Club

The first Conservative Club was established at 30 Bangor Street in the latter part of the nineteenth century with George William Duff Assheton Smith as president. As the result of his successor, Sir Charles Assheton Smith, donating a piece of land, roofing slate and the sum of £50, the opportunity was taken to build a new Club. Sir Charles also provided the secretary of the club with a list of names such as the Duke of Sutherland, Marquis of Salisbury, Earl of Lancaster and Duke of Northumberland, with authority to approach them for financial assistance in the erection of the building. [VP 3256]

When completed in 1914, even allowing for its political nature, it did provide a venue where entertainment could be staged. The whole of the first floor of the new club took the form of an assembly room where a variety of events were held including dances, film shows, concerts, whist drives and even a .22 rifle range. Soon after opening, Mr Codman, a well-known Llandudno entertainer, sought permission to show 'moving pictures' of the war once a month. Even though he was willing to share the admission fee with the parish council on a 50:50 basis his application was refused.

The silent films, or 'living pictures' as they were described, shown by R.D. Vaughan at the Conservative Club, or the Queens Cinema as it had been named, were well supported by the villagers even though cinemas, such as the Picturedrome in Bangor, provided a wider choice of film. Films were delivered to Port Dinorwic by car by Mr W. Lee who was involved with various Bangor cinemas. [NWC 6.7.1917] If there was a delay in the film's arrival then Mr Vaughan would announce to the waiting audience that his daughter Susie would perform a song and dance until it arrived! To accompany the silent films and to set the mood for the changing scenes, a local pianist provided the appropriate 'mood' music. The film performance would last for just over an hour and at the end he would announce 'next week we have Charlie Chaplin in two parts!'

A break in the fragile film was a regular occurrence in most cinemas but Vaughan had an additional problem with the electricity supply. Since the chloride batteries used for storing the electricity produced at the dry dock power house only had a limited holding capacity, he would be advised periodically by Mr Glover, the electrician responsible for the power house, that his projector 'was using excessive electricity'. This could be to the detriment of other users of electrical appliances in the village. At the time of a coal strike during the 1920s, Vaughan was informed by Mr Glover: 'owing to a shortage of coal, I shall be unable to supply you with power for your cinema shows only on two evenings a week'. The first floor assembly room was eventually converted into a flat for the caretaker in 1934 and therefore no further events were held there.

If there was reluctance on the part of keen local billiard and snooker players to participate in the Conservative Club's facilities, more especially the two snooker tables, for political reasons, there were three other venues in the village with similar facilities including the Halfway House Inn which had held a billiards licence since the latter part of the nineteenth century. The YMCA, which was established in 1905 in a house at the bottom of Port Terrace, was later relocated to 71 Bangor Street where two billiard tables were available. The YMCA was closed in the mid 1950s. The fourth venue was the basement of the Eiffel café run by Robert Williams and his sister, Grace, where a table had been installed primarily no doubt to encourage patronage of the café.

Memorial Hall

One of the main events in the village calendar was the annual three-day eisteddfod. The decision was taken for it to be held at the Memorial Hall, rather than at the Bryn Menai Chapel where it had been established and ensured plenty of support due to its central position in the village. Another event held annually for the benefit of the children was the Rose Queen festival. Other periodic events such as *Snow White* or *Fourteen Merry Men* produced by ladies of the village, were staged over three nights with all the staging, props and costumes made locally.

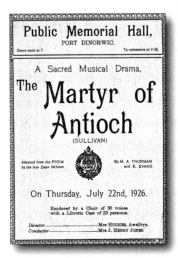

The hall also proved to be a popular venue with numerous organisations, including the local youth club, *Clwb y Fenai*, which gave members the opportunity to participate in Red Cross classes, dancing, badminton, boxing, weight lifting and judo. Other organisations that local youth could join were the Boy Scouts, Girl Guides, Sea Scouts and Wolf Cubs.

Outdoor events were also popular, especially football, cricket and tennis. Although attempts had been made towards the end of

Memorial Hall drama 1920. [Bethan Smith]

Clwb y Fenai girls' choir 1945 [Bethan Smith]
Top: Rhianon Jones; Mona Pritchard; Nancy
Williams; Vona Williams; Betty Pierce
Davies; Jean Howard; Mona Mai Williams;
Dilys Owen. Middle: Sylvia Williams; Ella
Carr; Eileen Hughes Jones; Bessie Orwig
Jones; Maimie Noel Jones; Olive Gardner;
Betty Williams. Front: Violet Griffiths;
Brenda Lloyd Jones; Mair Price; Betty Jones;
Nancy Hughes

Left: Clwb y Fenai members 1952.
[Mair Jones]

Clwb y Fenai members having competed at the
eisteddfod. [Loreta Evans]
Back L–R: Maimie Noel Jones (accompanist);
Buddyg Hughes; Esther Dop; Loreta Bowles;
Joyce Roberts; Doris Pierce; Nesta Pierce.
Front: Lorna Woodfine; Marian Thomas;
Betty Jones; Dilys Jones; Margaret Roberts;
Vera Humphreys.

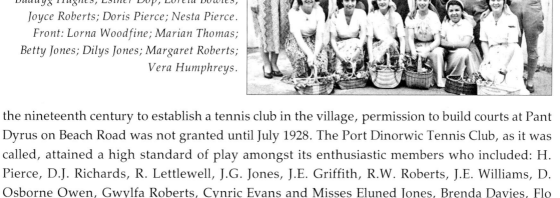

the nineteenth century to establish a tennis club in the village, permission to build courts at Pant Dyrus on Beach Road was not granted until July 1928. The Port Dinorwic Tennis Club, as it was called, attained a high standard of play amongst its enthusiastic members who included: H. Pierce, D.J. Richards, R. Lettlewell, J.G. Jones, J.E. Griffith, R.W. Roberts, J.E. Williams, D. Osborne Owen, Gwylfa Roberts, Cynric Evans and Misses Eluned Jones, Brenda Davies, Flo Horlock, Dilys Hughes, Nora Owen, Lettie Pierce and Della Pierce. Such was the keenness of some members that shoppers were occasionally confronted by a notice on a shop door stating 'Gone to tennis – back in an hour!' Attempts were also made to establish a bowling green either alongside the tennis courts or in the field adjoining the station, but both failed.

Cricket was certainly encouraged and a pavilion at Brynadda was donated by Sir Michael Duff. The local team was formed from the unemployed and established by Osborne Owen from the

Port Dinorwic Tennis Club members 1930s.
[John Richards] Standing: Mair Jones;
Florrie Horlock; Vina Davies; Gwyneth
Williams. Seated: Mona Williams; Ellen
Pierce; Muriel Horlock; Dilys Hughes.

Midland Bank. When a player attained a certain level of proficiency, he would be transferred to the main team which had been established in 1934 under the captaincy of Tommy Jones, Terfyn Terrace. Not only were they allowed to play in the grounds of Vaynol but were also permitted to call themselves the Vaynol Cricket Club. Invariably, the men were accompanied by lady supporters who were not only responsible for the refreshments but also took care of the scoring. The same level of support was given whether they played at Parkia or Plas Newydd which, in the latter case, entailed being taken by ferry at 1d per head, to play against Lord Anglesey and friends.

Football was played wherever a piece of ground was available. Reclaimed land at Pant Dyrus on Beach Road although far from ideal, was popular with youngsters who played in whatever clothing they were wearing. Even though it was impossible to distinguish between the two teams, it made no difference since most of the players having been through the mud to retrieve the ball from the sea a number of times would finish the game the same colour. Playing conditions were far better for those allowed to play on the Cefn Farm field or the Glyn field held by Robert Owen of the Halfway Inn.

Griffith Ellis, secretary of the Conservative Club and a keen supporter of local sport, made an approach to the Vaynol estate agent, R.P. Harding, in the 1920s for the use of a field. A letter from the

Above: Port Dinorwic YMCA football team 1930–1.

Port Dinorwic football team 1930s.

Trustees of Vaynol Estate 'consented to give the Club members the use of Brynadda Field to play football on Saturday after-noons [members] will abide by the Rules laid down'. Although a similar agreement had been in existence since 1899, never-theless, it still had to be negotiated annually. [GAS VP3391] When the match was due to be played against Bangor at Vaynol Park on 3 January 1925, the captain had the task of deciding on the team from the following

Port Dinorwic football team 1948–9.

players: Hugh Owen, Evie Evans, Hugh Pritchard, R. Williams, J. Roderick, W.J. Hughes, W.R. Williams, J. Jones, Tom Lewis, R. Allman, J. Davies, Harry Hughes and M. Hughes.

Many towns and villages in Caernarfonshire had a brass or silver band and Felinheli was no exception. The first brass band, with William Jones as bandmaster, was established in the village in 1865 and, prior to holding a concert of instrumental music in the National School in December of that year, the bandmaster approached Mr R.G. Duff Assheton Smith of Vaynol for permission to include his name on the programme as patron. In a reply sent to his agent Millington, he said 'I do not know anything about the Port Dinorwic Brass Band but if it is a thing to be encouraged I have no objection to allow my name to be put on their programme as patron'. [GAS VP 2669] In later years, the Port Dinorwic Brass Band came under the baton of Patrick Ayres.

As far as singing was concerned, the local male voice choir, conducted by Robert Williams, would practise at the Halfway House Inn to the accompaniment of a portable harmonium which, when required, would be carried from Williams's home.

Entertainment

During the course of the year, villagers were well provided with a variety of itinerant entertainers including a man who was accompanied by a performing brown bear and a woman who provided an exhibition of 1920s dancing on a piece of wood in the street, with music provided by her partner playing a piano accordion. Travelling drama companies performed plays such as *Murder in the Red Barn* or *Sweeney Todd* wherever a stage was available. However, the local repertory company were just as accomplished, enthralling audiences with *Hobson's Choice* and many other dramas, with dedicated supporters dealing with the wardrobe, staging and lighting.

In the twentieth century, the names of Simons, Teago or Wildman were associated with the world of travelling shows throughout north Wales. *Sioe Simons* paid an annual visit to the village and was set up on Beach Road. It was an event that everyone, young and old of the village, looked forward to.

Thomas Henry Charles Teago, whose father was a publican in Bristol, suffered from ill-health and was advised by his doctor to move further north. When he knew that a Mr A. Wildman, an established showman, was travelling in that direction, he decided, like many other youngsters in those days, to run away from home and sample the nomadic life. They travelled through Wales in the latter part of the nineteenth century and eventually settled in Caernarfon. Wildman obtained a lease to stage shows in the Pavilion, including roller skating on a maple wood floor. An advertisement in the *Carnarvon & Denbigh Herald* for 8 August 1898 gave details of his stage show which included the Waenfawr Brass Band (which had won first prize at the Llangefni eisteddfod the previous year). Prices were 3s, 2s, 1s and 6d 'children half price except to 6d seats'. [GAS XM642] The advertisement also provided times of late night trains to Port Dinorwic and Llanberis as well as the time of the ferry boat service to Anglesey for those returning home.

When Wildman retired from the business in 1911, he took over the Blue Bell Hotel in Conwy and Thomas Teago continued with both the Pavilion winter show and the travelling fair, assisted by his son who was also named Tom. This partnership continued until Thomas senior retired from the fairground to take over the Prince of Wales Vaults in Menai Bridge circa 1915.

With the Teago and Simons families on the road during the summer months, it was inevitable that they would meet from time to time at the same show ground and during such an encounter that the brother and sister, Edward and Emma Simons met the brother and sister Tom and Clara Teago. Consequently Edward married Clara and Tom married Emma.

When John Simons died, his wife and son, Edward (one of eleven children), continued with the fair which, by now, was showing slides with a bioscope or by magic lantern. To country folk, whose knowledge of the outside world was very limited, the pictures produced on the screen would enthral everyone who flocked to view these unbelievable sights. After a season of showing the pictures in towns and villages, the slides were exchanged for more up-to-date material. When silent films replaced the slide show, Edward Simons supplied the background or mood music by playing a violin, provided that there was someone else available to handle the projector.

To justify the admission price, further attractions were introduced such as side shows, swings and roundabouts, together with a concert platform where jugglers, impersonators, vocalists and dancers were seen. Members of the Simons family, namely Daisy and Amy, also participated as dancers.

By 1910, the Simons show had grown to such an extent that traction engines instead of horses hauled the trailers and caravans, including those that housed the men employed to handle the equipment. These engines, which were slow and cumbersome, gave a lot of problems when

Green's Bantams. [Tilda Ryan]

Raging Cockerels. [Tilda Ryan]

negotiating certain roads such as that around Penmaenmawr or descending hills when wooden blocks were ever ready to be placed under the wheels of both the engine and trailers, especially in wintry conditions. The steep approaches to the Pant Dyrus site at Beach Road in Felinheli, where the show was sited, presented problems. This was overcome to a certain extent by descending the Halfway House

Teago's traction engine Matilda. *[Tilda Ryan]*

hill to the quay and through the gate at the bottom of Snowdon Street. As well as having greater pulling power, these engines also had the ability to generate direct-current electricity. Not only was this essential for show-ground equipment, but it also provided a mass of coloured lights which were an attraction in themselves, particularly to people who were used to the dim light of a candle, paraffin lamp, or at best, gas light. The procession of trailers, including one that comfortably housed the family, covered most of the towns and villages between Rhyl and Criccieth before entertaining inland places.

The duration of visits to towns and villages was usually based largely on the catchment area and on previous experiences. Advance notice of their visits was given by posters printed by Gwenlyn Evans at Caernarfon. More often than not, the same site was used each year such as a field where Glyn House in Bangor is now located and which at that time was also used by the City Football Club. As the years went by and sites were built upon, it became increasingly difficult to find a suitable place to stage their shows.

With the approach of winter, Teago invariably leased the Pavilion in Caernarfon until March or April of the following year in order that the fairground could avoid the worst of the weather. For a price, he would allow any other showman, such as Simons, a space for his stalls or equipment within the pavilion.

All the travelling fairs came off the road on the outbreak of the First World War and the equipment was stored in a yard in Birkenhead while the men were in the forces. Entertainment in Caernarfon Pavilion also ended when the army took over the building for billeting soldiers in about 1916 and for the next two years, Teago continued with shows and entertainment, albeit restricted to bobby-horses and small stalls in the cold 'Kiwi' building on St Helens Road which belonged to Morris & Jones. With the ending of the war, he returned to the Pavilion where he continued with his winter shows until the outbreak of the Second World War.

In 1915, Simons decided to open a cinema in Abergele. This enabled him to travel in the summer months and spend winter off the road. After ten years, he decided to finish with the travelling show as cinemas were opening in most towns and the travelling cinema had lost its original appeal.

Edward Simons with his Magic Lantern. [Tilda Ryan]

The working partnership between Edward Simons and Henry Teago, which lasted for about three years (1922–5), ended when the former decided to settle in Rhyl at the time when the Marine Lake complex was just starting.

The *Carnarvon & Denbigh Herald* gave details of a Grand Complimentary Benefit Night held in the 1930s to celebrate Mr Teago's tenancy of the pavilion. It was described as the 'Night of all Nights'. The admission fee, described as the 'Largest Three Penny Worth in Life' provided the audience with merry-go-rounds, fortune-tellers, skating rink, trapeze artists, balancing acts, illusionists and hypnotists as well as the 'Potters of the Flying Rollers' who came every year, Ormonde and Lord; cycle act, the Loc Hoc Tschn acrobatic troop and Madame A. Hengeluer dog act. Posters advertising these events were placed in forty different locations in Caernarfon, ranging from public houses to fish and chip shops.

As a consequence of having disposed of their equipment, and their personnel being enrolled in the forces at the start of the Second World War, the travelling fair became confined to static shows at such places as the Caernarfon Pavilion when available.

In complete contrast to fairground thrills, the flying circuses toured the country directly after the First World War, providing the public with an opportunity to observe stunt flying. Idwal ap Ieuan Jones of Talysarn, having learnt to fly with the RAF in 1925, later joined the Sir Alan Cobham flying circus and three years later the C.W. Scott circus. Aerobatic exhibitions were given with planes such as the Avro 504 and the Flying Flea. An event held at Parkia fields near Griffith's Crossing in about 1930 enabled those keen to experience flying to do so in an Avro 504 biplane at a cost of five shillings.

Assheton Smith yachts

Thomas Assheton Smith (1776–1858) was an all-round sportsman and a particularly good cricketer having made forty-five appearances in first class cricket up to 1820. He had a life-long enthusiasm for sailing and during the many years that he had been a member of the Royal Yacht Club, he built no fewer than five sailing yachts. He was as equally competent in both the designing and building of steam yachts. This interest put him on a collision course with the traditionalists at the Admiralty who were totally against the introduction of steam. In 1829, the Royal Yacht Squadron, (whose members included many senior naval officers), decided that no gentleman owning a steam vessel could be a member. Thomas Assheton Smith resigned. This situation continued until 1856 when, as the result of increasing interest being shown in steam vessels, the Royal Yacht Squadron decided to allow individuals who owned steam yachts to be members.

The first steam yacht built by Robert Napier of Glasgow, the *Menai*, had the benefit of three keels to prevent rolling and cost £20,000. Subsequent steam yachts that Napier built in accordance with Assheton Smith's designs were:

	Name	Tonnage	Engine	Material
1830	*Menai*	400	120 h.p.	wood
1838	*Glowworm*	300	100 h.p.	iron
1840	*Fire-King*	700	230 h.p.	wood
1844	*Fire-Queen 1*	110	30 h.p.	iron
1845	*Fire-Queen 2*	230	80 h.p.	iron
1846	*Fire-Queen 3*	300	120 h.p.	iron
1847	*Jenny Lind*	220	70 h.p.	iron
1851	*Sea Serpent*	250	80 h.p.	iron

George William Duff Assheton Smith (1848–1904) did not have quite the enthusiasm for steam yachts as his uncle, Thomas Assheton Smith, nevertheless he acquired a yacht in 1866 called *Vaynol II*, built by R. Napier & Sons of the Vulcan Foundry in Glasgow. Measuring 75ft overall and having a 65ft deck, he described the vessel as 'a very pretty toy, but rather an expensive one as the manufacturers, Napier, made a mistake in the estimate'. By 1869, he was keen to dispose of her and his agent, Millington, wrote a letter to the builders asking if they knew of anyone likely to purchase her and stating that she was in excellent order. A further letter was sent in September 1869 asking 'if £800 would be a reasonable figure but advertising at £1,000'. The yacht's speed averaged eight knots and she used 1½ cwt. of coal per hour. She was eventually sold for £650 in December 1869. [GAS VP2379]

As George Assheton Smith was keen to explore the arctic, he purchased the SY *Pandora*, in 1882 an auxiliary three-masted barquentine of 388 tons gross built at Pembroke dockyard in 1867 as the gunboat *Newport* and which had been specially 'strengthened and fitted by the previous owner for arctic navigation'. [GAS VP4946] The crew of the *Pandora* was the same as that of the *Vaynol*, namely Owen Davies, master (his monthly wage was £8); Mark Hughes, fireman £7 (28 days at five shillings per day); Hugh Williams, engineer £5 12s 0d (28 days at four shillings per day); Henry Williams and William Williams, seamen £5 12s 4d each. [GAS VP4487]

Charles Garden Duff Assheton Smith (1815–1914) purchased the twin-masted, iron screw schooner SY *Amalthea* in 1907. She measured 189.3ft x 27.1ft x 15.0ft and had been built by Ramage & Ferguson at Leith in 1881. Her engine consisted of three furnaces which produced a working pressure of 80lbs. *Amalthea* was a familiar sight in the Port Dinorwic dock or anchored on the Menai Strait. Whilst she was in his possession, certain design changes were carried out to the stern and promenade deck by Cox & King, the London based naval architects, and at the same time a new smoking room was added. [GAS DQ3008, 3467, 3480]

She was requisitioned by the Admiralty at the start of the First World War and was based at the naval base at Stornoway and her name was changed to HMS *Iolaire*. At the end of the war, men from the Isle of Lewis, many of whom had been away in the services since the beginning of the conflict, were anxious to get home to be with their families and to celebrate Hogmanay. Having travelled by train, initially to Inverness and then to Kyle, arrangements were made for the HMS *Iolaire* to be sent from Stornoway to Kyle to assist in the transfer of the men to Stornoway. When *Iolaire* cast off on the 31 December 1918, she was reputedly carrying 190 servicemen but only eighty life-jackets and lifeboats for 100 men. The weather forecast was for a reasonable trip but by 00.30 hours the wind was freshening and the vessel encountered squalls and drizzling rain. In Stornoway harbour HM Drifter *Budding Rose* was waiting for the *Iolaire*, to act as her pilot-boat but, as a result of seeing a rocket fired at about 01.55 hours, her captain went to investigate and found the vessel in distress. Sadly, no assistance could be provided as the *Iolaire* was on the rocks and there were heavy seas running. According to subsequent inquiry reports, the *Iolaire* had missed the harbour entrance in the darkness, even though lights were being shown. Of the 284 men aboard the *Iolaire* only seventy-nine survived.

Port Dinorwic Regatta

There is no certainty as to when the first Port Dinorwic Annual Regatta was held, but a gravestone at Llanfairisgaer cemetery bears the wording: 'This stone is erected by the Port Dinorwic Regatta Committee to mark their appreciation of his public spirit'. It refers to George Edward Griffiths (1827–1901) who, after being at sea for a few years, became a smith at the Vaynol estate quay yard, subsequent to his having served the necessary apprenticeship. No record exists as to the reason for the accolade mentioned on the gravestone, but it does confirm that a local regatta committee was in existence prior to the turn of the century. Apart from the two world wars and the few occasions when adverse weather caused it to be cancelled, the regatta has been held annually ever since.

As is obvious from the size of the craft and the costs involved, yachting was generally confined to landowners and wealthy families. The 1909 Annual Regatta programme gives an indication of the size of craft then participating. The yachts listed for the first race of the day were: exceeding 15 tons – *Mayflower* (24 tons), *Almida* (24 tons), *Molita* (19 tons), *Anselma* (18 tons), *Wallaroo* (25 tons) and *Kathleen* (18 tons). The second race was confined to yachts not exceeding 15 tons including *Irene II* 15 tons, *Margaret* 9 tons, *Leda* 5 tons, *Darling III* 12 tons and *Mermaid* 9 tons. The programme specified that this was a 'Handicap Race for yachts belonging to and steered by a member of any Recognised Yacht Club'. All the boats mentioned usually carried a crew of five or more which was composed of local men who had the necessary expertise and knowledge of the strait's idiosyncratic tides and eddies. Other yachts that participated were from the Royal Anglesey Yacht Club, Royal Mersey Restricted Yacht Class and the West Lancashire Yacht Club.

Port Dinorwic Regatta 1909. [J. Heber Owen]

Regatta c.1910.

W.H. Rowland had established a boat-building business on the opposite side of the Afon Seiont to Caernarfon Castle in 1900, before moving to Bangor where he described himself as a 'Yacht, Launch and Boat Builder, Designer &c'. The various boats that he built included 'Sea Birds' half-raters and, according to the 1909 Port Dinorwic Regatta programme, three of these, *Chila*, *Mallard* and *Skua*, participated in the fifth race of the day.

Smaller yachts that raced on the day were described as 'Open Sailing Boats not exceeding 14 feet' including *Blanche* (J. Pierce Jones), *Hywel*, (H. Roberts) *Laura*, (O. Roberts) and *Swift* (R.D. Vaughan). Other races were for 'Boats belonging to Vessels which load Slates at Port Dinorwic Quay'.

The two local teams in the four-oared gigs race not only competed against each other, they also had rivals from Bangor and Caernarfon to contend with. The team representing the dry dock workers were Harold Roberts or Richard Dennis as coxswain together, with John McGuire, Evan Evans and William Griffith, and their gig had been built in about 1934 by Matthew Owen of Menai Bridge. The quay team raced

Port Dinorwic Regatta, 1909. [J. Heber Owen]

in a gig built by Price, a boat builder from Bangor, and included Lewis Griffith as coxswain, Owen Jones as stroke, Richard McGuire, Fred Jones, Hugh Williams and Owen Emrys Hughes as bowmen.

Local youngsters were also given the opportunity of displaying their skills in sculling, open punt and shovel races as well as participating in a 'swimming match'.

The Dinorwic Quarry ship SS *Enid* not only acted as flag ship for the 1909 regatta, but also had the honour of being the last Dinorwic Quarry ship to act as flagship in the 1951 regatta

The crowds that attended the regatta over the years not only enjoyed the yachting spectacle,

*Regatta day 1910 –
sculling races.
[Len Williams]*

many were attracted by the peripheral shore events, including the opportunity in purchasing the famous edible rock and competing for the prize of a leg of lamb for the person that success-fully reached the top of the greasy pole . Although yacht racing is as popular as ever, the number of spectators attending the annual regatta have declined considerably.

Port Dinorwic Sailing Club

In Port Dinorwic retired master mariners, who had served the greater part of their lives aboard sailing ships, were content to sail small dinghies which sported a burgee showing a white cross on a blue background and the initials PDYC, or even sail model yachts on the Strait. The old quay barracks, now long gone, was used as their clubhouse or 'headquarters'.

Sailing, once the prerogative of the rich, gradually changed during the twentieth century when a huge variety of craft became available at affordable prices. Directly after the Second World War, local sailing enthusiasts began racing at Corbett's Bay where the 'officials' on shore had the benefit of a table and two chairs borrowed from a nearby house and an old 'station clock' for time-keeping. It may well have been that such seemingly 'unprofessional method of conducting yacht racing' resulted in a meeting being held at the Memorial Hall on 23 June 1947 for 'Yacht and Boat

*Regatta Queen Jean,
1952. [Jean Hughes]*

Regatta Queen Pearl, with Sir Michael and Lady Caroline, 1950. [Pearl Heald]

owners and others interested'. This inaugural meeting decided that a sailing club would be formed, to be called the Port Dinorwic Sailing Club (PDSC), and that members would agree to race under the Yacht Club Association (YCA) rules. Such participation allowed the club to compete against others racing under the same association rules. In July 1947, it was decided that the new club's burgee should be a Red Dragon on a green background with the letters PDSC and, at a later meeting, it was decided that the Dragon should be rampant (rearing or standing in profile on the left hind leg) rather than passant (standing with three paws on the ground and one paw raised). The annual membership fee was set at 5/- (25p).

With an increasing club membership, it was decided to acquire a clubhouse and, with an abundance of structures in the area to choose from directly after the war, it was eventually decided to purchase a hut for £75 from RAF Bodorgan. It was erected near the pre-war tennis court at Pant Dyrus by the firm of Dowsett Mackay (see Wartime chapter).

A meeting of the Sailing Committee and prospective purchasers of new boats met at the office of Roberts & Sons on 10 February 1948 to discuss the new Brooke Marine designed 16-foot yacht which could be purchased at a cost of £300 'with full speci-fication'. Since the price was considered to be too high, it was decided that the assistance of the Yacht Racing Association should be sought in locating about seven second-hand

Port Dinorwic One-Design yacht Gypsy *at Moel-y-Don jetty. [Emyr Wyn Roberts]*

boats, priced at about £150 each, of the same size and design to allow for competitive racing. On 24 February, an offer was received from P. Waters & Son of Appledore in Devon to supply three boats, to be known as the Port Dinorwic One-Design (PDOD), at a price of £130 18s 10d.

The first 16-foot PDOD yacht to arrive in the village was the boat to be named *Fulmar* (acquired by D.I. Lloyd) which was clinker built with bowsprit and gunter rig and a heavy steel centre plate. With its small jib, large main and overhanging boom and no cleats, it was recorded that it was quite a handful to sail in any breeze especially on the run. It had been originally designed in 1905 by I.S. Marriott for the Taw and Torridge Sailing Club.

Three additional boats were ordered from Appledore and allocated to John Maguire (*Ellen*), Roberts Brothers (*Wyn*) and Alec Dancer (*Julia*). Inevitably, because of the variations in design between the PDOD boats (due to the builder not having a plan to work from), it was decided that any additional boats ordered would be built to exactly the same specifications as the original boat, namely, *Fulmar*. The next stage in standardisation occurred when Dr Henry Edwards purchased a new yacht in 1950 which met with the initial reaction that she should be banned from racing against the One-Design because of the differences in deck design, rig and boom. However, when a trial race was arranged between her (with Eric Owen at the helm) and the established Port Dinorwic One Design, the new boat won easily. On the strength of such a result, it was decided that the sails, booms and gaffs of all the boats would be modified to the same specifications as Dr Edwards's new boat thereby producing some semblance of uniformity. However, the inevitable variations in the boats, whether by design or later adaptation by the owners, produced unexpected results in performances which were not always to the benefit of the crews concerned.

At the first meeting of the sailing club held in the 'new' building, which consisted of the main room, kitchen and committee room, on 3 August 1948, their assets were listed as three cups, one stop-watch, three dozen packs of playing cards, one bell on stand, one gavel, and a registered burgee. Shortly after the clubhouse was opened by Sir Michael Duff on 16 November 1948, enquiries were being made regarding the possibility of holding functions in the building and it was decided that the playing of games such as darts, draughts, dominoes and cards should be allowed in the clubhouse but that any member found guilty of gambling should be expelled.

The contentious matter of the club applying for a 'licence to sell intoxicating drinks' was raised from time to time, but a meeting held on 18 March 1948 resolved 'to place on record that this matter is duly and finally decided' against making an application. The topic was still under discussion at the AGM held in 1975 when 'a vote decided by 26 to 8 and eight abstentions, against having a bar for various reasons including 'the question of who was going to be responsible for running it; security problems, cadet members and insurance premiums could be affected'. Perhaps this may have been the reason why executive committee members met at the Garddfon Inn from time to time?

Apart from the annual regatta with its strict rules for racing, individuals, especially youngsters, enjoyed pottering about in boats, especially during the summer months. In addition to running the ferry, Captain Tom Lillie bought a sailing boat by the name of *Vega* but the local sailing fraternity had a low opinion of its bamboo mast. A character by the name of Lewis Griffith Jones

Port Dinorwic yachts passing under the Menai Bridge c.1950.

reluctantly agreed to accompany Captain Lillie on *Vega's* maiden voyage and, while tacking in a strong breeze, the mast broke necessitating their having to row back to the jetty. The many observers to this event saw Jones walking up the jetty carrying his shoes and socks and muttering 'Captain Lillie and his bloody bamboo mast!'

Titus Roberts was another character who owned two vessels, named *Atomic* and *Thunderbolt* facetiously described as yachts. Although never actually sailing himself, he took great delight in watching local youngsters sailing them. More often than not, due to the fact that they tended to leak, more time was spent baling out than sailing.

Other yachts to be seen in the early years were: *Firecrest*, *Jewel*, *Breezy Ann*, *Gypsy*, *Skeed*, *Slip*, *Ellen*, *Red Diver* and *Jina*. In the post-war years, because material of every description was in short supply, some of the yachts resorted to making sails out of old flour bags. Since the name of the flour company: Rigby, Frost or National Flour could not be obliterated, on shore spectators were aware of their origin.

Rather than have their yachts identified from the shore by means of a number displayed on the sail, some of the owners brought individuality to sailing at Port Dinorwic by introducing coloured sails, e.g. *Fulmar* – green; *Gypsy* – blue; *Patsy* – red and *Thesia* – yellow. It was not unknown for one or two to dye the sails red by soaking them in cochineal in a large bath and then hanging them to dry. However, as soon as they were subjected to adverse weather conditions the dye was transferred from sail to members of the crew.

With increasing numbers of both yachts and races came the question of safety. Initially the sailing committee felt that it would be sufficient that 'each boat must carry lifebelts or life-jackets in an accessible place for each person on board' but a further decision taken in March 1948 stated that the wearing of life-savers would be compulsory.

Within four years, races were being held on Wednesday evenings as well as Saturday afternoons between May and September. With an increasing number of boats participating in the races by 1952, it was agreed that the remaining monies held in the Jetty Fund would be used to purchase a rescue boat – *Pat II*. Later as the result of this vessel developing a leak and liable to be out of commission at a time of emergency, a Dell Quay Dory was purchased instead at a cost of £300.

As the number of boats requiring storage during the winter months increased, a request was made for the tennis court to be made available for this purpose (the court had been badly damaged during the war when it was used for storing Dow-Mac material). This was agreed but that the club would have to vacate it if the court was repaired during the winter.

Boat owners and yachts in 1957 were:

W.N. Owen	*Patsy*	J.M. Jones	*Julia* N°· 3
E.G. Davies	*Ymkin*	O.G. Roberts	*Wyn*
Dr H. Edwards	*Thesia* N°· 8	A.R. Blakeley	*Elaine*
Dr E. Rowlands	*Gypsy* N°· 5	D.I. Lloyd	*Fulmar* N°· 4

In the early days of the club, invidious rules were introduced such as: 'At a meeting held 6 December 1963 it was decided that all club officials and members of the executive committee must be resident within 20 miles (and that) the term residence refers to the main place of residence and excludes all form of holiday and week-end residence'. Other forms of parochialism occurred with regard to conduct within the club house when a member agreed to be secretary provided that 'the Sailing Club does not countenance nor sanction Sunday racing under auspices of the Club'.

The matter of being able to communicate between the shore and the rescue boat by means of a Walkie-Talkie was discussed. A few years later an Aldis lamp for signalling was being considered. Eventually, in 1988 it was decided that hand radios would be purchased at a price of £263.

A new club house was under consideration in 1970 at an estimated cost of £9,700 and a possible Welsh Office grant of £3,790 was being considered by Goronwy Roberts, MP (later Lord Goronwy Roberts). This was eventually approved and within a few months, the new building had been erected. From being a very parochial and restrictive organisation, the sailing club had by then become far more democratic and cosmopolitan with the removal of restrictive rules.

10: SECOND WORLD WAR

Preparations for war – emergency services

In 1938 when war appeared to be inevitable, preparations were made to enrol personnel for the emergency services such as Air Raid Precautions (ARP), Women's Voluntary Service (WVS), Women's Institute (WI), Auxiliary Fire Service, Red Cross and St John's Ambulance. The first indication of the seriousness of the situation became apparent when posters appeared at various locations within the village advising individuals where and when gas masks would be made available for everyone irrespective of age. For the duration of the war, the ubiquitous brown box containing the gas mask was a constant companion irrespective of time or location.

With the threat of a German invasion, particularly after the evacuation of military forces from Dunkirk between 26 May and 4 June 1940, Anthony Eden, Minister of War, made a radio appeal on 14 May for men between the ages of seventeen and sixty-five who were either ineligible for military service due to age or occupation, or were yet to be enrolled in the forces, to join the Local Defence Volunteers. Between the time of the radio appeal and August 1940, 1.5 million men had joined the Home Guard as it was later renamed (the organisation remained active until December 1944).

Evacuation

With the knowledge that cities such as Manchester and Liverpool could well suffer from air raids, preparations were made for the evacuation of children to those north Wales towns and villages which were less likely to suffer the anticipated bombing attacks. Lists were prepared in May 1939 of the names of children who would be evacuated, together with the station of departure. Parental authority for evacuated children to receive medical treatment, if or when necessary, was also obtained. To further assist, and possibly persuade parents of the wisdom of allowing their children to be evacuated, a handbook entitled *Air Raid Precautions and Evacuation 1939* was provided to each household which contained details of the method of dispersal by train or bus .

On 1 September 1939, children and teachers evacuated from Heyworth Street School in Liverpool arrived by train at Port Dinorwic. Standing on the station platform, the children looked dazed and bewildered as to where they were. A few clutched small cases, others a pillow case with a few pieces of clothing, whilst the remainder had only their gas box and the clothes that they were wearing. The label that each child had tied to their jacket lapel gave their name and that of their school. They were taken initially to the Memorial Hall from where they were allocated to families in the village. [GAS EA9/5] The task of finding accommodation for the evacuees fell on the shoulders of the two headmasters, D.J. Rowlands and John Owen.

Evacuee children at Glan Menai, Port Dinorwic, c.1940 preparing for potato planting. [W. Wyn Roberts]

The education of the evacuated children presented a problem because of the numbers involved and the local Council and National schools had difficulty coping with the extra pupils.

Council School
5 September 1939: First batch of evacuees (Heyworth Street) arrived from Liverpool. School remained closed owing to a large number of evacuees.
11 September 1939: School reopened. The two shift system will be worked. During the first week the local children will receive instructions till 12.45 and from 1.15–5 p.m. the visiting school (Earle Road Senior Girls – Miss Haslam, headmistress) will attend. The Earle Road scholars number about 150 (later the programme was changed to 9–12 and 1–4).
3 November 1939: The number of evacuees has greatly diminished. Originally there were 172 in the school but less that 100 remain.
27 November 1939: Resumed full time school. One of the classrooms has been placed at the disposal of the visiting children; the remainder of Earle Road children are at the Hall (Memorial) and Elim vestry. [GAS XES1/103/3 5]

National School
11 September 1939: Double shift system – Heyworth Street Council School admitted 16 children who are voluntary evacuees staying with relatives at Port Dinorwic.
18 September 1939: Gas masks drill – fitting at the Memorial Hall. ARP Red Alerts sounded periodically.
2 September 1941: Cyril Rowlands, BSc, RNVR, son of the Head Master and former pupil, stationed at Malta awarded the George Medal. He later received a bar to his medal as a bomb disposal officer. Armistice Day recognised in schools [GAS XES1/73/2 1913-1942]
17 April 1945: A pupil from the school, Robin Dop, aged 6, was fatally injured while playing on the beach road near his home. A large iron structure (a section of one of many barges being built at Dinas by Dowsett-Mackay – Brooke Marine) fell on him and killed him instantly.
19.4.1945: Funeral of the above named. School closed. Headmaster and pupils attended the funeral both at the house and churchyard. [GAS XES1/73/3]

In an attempt at reducing the disruption to the education of both local children and the evacuees, use was made of Elim Chapel vestry and the Memorial Hall.

By November 1939, possibly due to the absence of war-like activity, there was a tendency for children to start returning to Liverpool, particularly at weekends, and records showed that the number still at the village had decreased. However, with the commencement of the bombing and its consequences, additional children were evacuated from Liverpool during 1941.

When the 'mothers and babies' evacuee contingent arrived from Liverpool and other places, they were given accommodation in Plas Llanfair and the Memorial Hall where centralised facilities were provided for around one hundred individuals. Bedding had been stored at the Arvonia shop months before war broke out in anticipation of such an emergency. With so many babies to be bathed, hot water had to be carried from the Church House each day. The WVS had the added responsibility of providing them with food.

Since many of the evacuated children came from very poor families, they had no alternative clothing or footwear. To overcome this problem, an application had to be made for supplementary coupons in order that clothing could be purchased. When boots required repairing, assuming that leather was available, it meant that the wearer had no alternative but to stay indoors until their footwear was returned.

The weekly billeting allowances relating to evacuated children in 1942 were: aged under 5 years 8s 6d; 5–10 years 10s 6d; 10–12 years 11s; 12–14 years 12s; 14–16 years 13s; 16 years 15s 6d; 17 years and over 16s 6d. Further assistance was given with free midday meals but this depended on the number in the family and income. The same criteria applied with the free distribution of halibut liver oil capsules and iron tablets. If they had to be paid for then the cost was 2d per week for the capsules and 1d for the tablets. Just before Christmas, the City of Liverpool made an evacuation allowance of 2s per child to cover extras over the festivities.

Most parents of evacuated children were anxious about their welfare and would naturally correspond on a regular basis. However, if contact was not maintained, the City of Liverpool Education Department would investigate and the explanation given by some mothers was that the father had been in prison.

Rationing

The inconvenience of the rationing of food, petrol, clothing and other material was grudgingly accepted and it was invariably the unfortunate shopkeeper who had to stand the housewife's wrath and she in turn had to face a grumbling family that was being subjected to a strict discipline with regard to quantity of items such as sugar, tea, cooking fat, fruit etc that could be bought. Perhaps the least inconvenienced by such wartime conditions were the poorer families whose choice and quantity was governed not by rationing, but by the amount of money they had available.

With so much of food and basic materials needed to sustain life being imported, availability was governed not solely by rationing but by the number of ships that were able to avoid enemy attacks and arrive safely at a British port.

Cars were still regarded as luxury items at the start of the war and were available to only a few. Due to the shortage of petrol and the difficulty in maintaining the vehicles, most owners took them off the road and placed them in store for the duration of hostilities. Petrol was only available to a few essential users, such as doctors, but even then it was severely rationed. Even Sir Michael Duff, invalided out of the Royal Air Force in 1944, had to make a similar request for petrol coupons in order that he could attend to the estate and public duties.

At the outbreak of war, the gardens of Vaynol came under the category of a 'private garden' and Ogwen Rural District Council granted a licence for surplus vegetables to be distributed to local people. It was stated that the gardens had never been run for profit but that a large part of the produce was given to charity, fetes and good causes in connection with the war effort. A letter to the War Agriculture Committee in Caernarfon in 1944 pointed out firmly that if this situation was unacceptable, then Sir Michael would not distribute any more garden produce which would be a loss to the public.

Restrictions

Fishing, yachting and general pleasure boat activities were severely restricted during the war as a permit was required before a boat could be launched. According to a letter written in June 1942 by a person from the village seeking such a permit, the observation was made possibly by the Caernarvon Harbour Master:

> John Jones is very fond of yachting. As this is prohibited at the moment he has converted his craft into a fishing boat. Capt. Thomas does not believe that Jones does any fishing but pretends to do so as to obtain a licence in order that he can take his boat out.

If the claim were true, fishing supplemented a meagre diet brought about by rationing or lack of money. [GAS XD15 30/95]

Licences were issued to the following under the category of 'Rowboat Rosters' on 30 September 1942:

		Permit No.
John Jones, 1 Rhyd Fenai, Bush Road	*Lark* 16ft	M102
Morris Thomas, 10 Beach Road	*Tom* 10ft	M114
T. Preston, Tynewydd	*Dot* 13ft	M116
William Owen, 4 Jubilee Terrace	*Jet*	M120
Roberts & Sons	*Pip* 10ft	M123
J. Smallwood, Gwaithdy	*Squib* 12ft	M125
J. Tildsley, Bryn Melyn	*Betty* 13ft	M129
A.E. Williams, Westfields	*Pip*	M133
W.J. Parry, 24 Seaview Terrace	*Jean* 14ft & *Nigger* 18ft	M138
W.E. Parker, Old Shipyard	*Pram* 10ft	M141
Col. R.R. Davies, Min y Garth, Glyn Garth	*Anne* 14ft	M142
O.T. Williams, Plas Dinorwic	*Wren* 10ft	M152
R.J. Bowles, 18 Beach Road	*Leslie* 12ft	M153

Military Occupation

As a result of Vaynol Hall and the surrounding buildings and grounds being requisitioned, the 29th British General Hospital, Royal Army Medical Corp took it over after their arrival from Egypt in December 1943.

Women's Services

Of the twenty or so members of the Women's Land Army working at Vaynol, some were involved with the farm or garden while others worked for the forestry department.

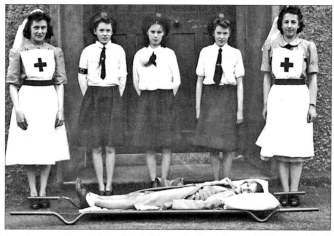

Junior members of the Port Dinorwic Red Cross. [Olive Bocking]

The Women's Voluntary Services were responsible for many of the services in the village during the war including running a small café, Berw House, on the corner of Port Terrace, established for the benefit of service men and women.

Fruit preservation was organised by the WVS and WI and supported by local chapels and churches with the end product gladly purchased by local shopkeepers to supplement their meagre supplies. The WVS and WI also assisted in the packing of parcels composed of various articles such as tinned goods, cigarettes and clothing supplied by the Red Cross for Allied prisoners-of war. Other items were added to supplement the parcels as and when funds were raised locally by the WVS and WI.

The Auxiliary Fire Service

The Arvonia shop was used as the headquarters of the local Auxiliary Fire Service unit and for storing the euphemistically described fire-fighting equipment which consisted of an old Vauxhall car with a ladder tied to its roof and a pump trailer on tow. On hearing a fire alarm, the village firemen would arrive in various states of attire depending on the time of day or night. The person in charge, since he did not have the luxury of living within walking distance of the headquarters, had to resort to a bicycle to give him a sporting chance of getting there before they left without him. More often than not, there was little chance of this happening since the time of departure for the fire unit was governed by the length of time it took to start the car engine.

Auxiliary Fire Service with Evie Evans, Rees Jones, County Fire Chief, Richard Allman and Jim Maxwell. [Emyr Owen]

*St John's Ambulance members
with Dr Gwilym ap Vychan Jones.
[Nell Thomas]
Back L–R: Mrs Lilian Jones,
Mrs Humphreys, Mrs Megan
Griffith, Mrs Laura Jones,
Mrs Katie Pierce Roberts.
Middle: Mrs Katie Jones,
Mrs Lewis Edwards, Dr ap
Vychan Jones, Mrs Gardner,
Mrs Robert Williams. Front:
Miss Gwyneth Hughes, Mrs Lily
Blanche Evans, Mrs Louise
Murray.*

Air Raid Wardens

Their main task was to ensure that no light was to be seen emanating from a window or doorway. One persistent offender regularly failed to close his curtains despite the pleading of the wardens. In the end, they resorted to throwing a stone at the window and broke the glass. No light was seen from then on. Even a cigarette smoker would not be tolerated out in the open at night. Such total darkness caused numerous problems with pedestrians colliding with objects and even with each other with dire consequences. Since most houses had their toilets at the bottom of the garden, a visit in the darkness was fraught with danger as the user sought the sanctuary of the *tŷ bach* by groping along the washing line while tripping over unexpected obstacles such as next door's cat. [GAS EA/9/5, XD1 266 1939–45]

Prisoners of War

German prisoners-of-war began arriving in Vaynol from a transit camp in southern England in September 1945. Even though most had not experienced farm work in civilian life, they worked alongside members of the Women's Land Army and local workers with whom they were popular because of their willingness and ability to tackle most jobs on the farm.

The camp, situated in the Vaynol forestry yard near to Capel Graig Lodge, consisted of three Nissan huts, housing twenty prisoners in each. The five soldiers who initially guarded them were eventually with-

*Women's Land Army members Betty
Kitto, Katie May Williams and Ann
Goodman with local farm workers and
German POWs at Vaynol c.1945.*

drawn and the prisoners were allowed to walk unescorted down to the village where they could see films at the Church House or even participate in occasional dances. They remained in Vaynol for approximately two and a half years whilst awaiting repatriation, but when the time came for them to be released and to return home, some of them decided to remain in this country.

German prisoners of war at Vaynol, 1947. [Ludger Lonnermann]

Sadly, many families suffered the loss of loved ones due to enemy action during the war but as far as the village was concerned, other than hearing the distinctive drone of German aircraft passing overhead at night, it saw nothing of the bombing that many towns and cities experienced. The well-organised evacuation of children to towns and villages in the country undoubtedly saved many lives and the safe haven that they found in Felinheli was a never-to-be

Celebrations in Bangor Street at the end of the Second World War. [Rhian Gwyn]

forgotten experience for the children and the families that cared for them. Many of the children maintained contact with the friends that they had made in the village after returning home.

11: SHIPBUILDING

The hamlet of Dinas was synonymous with ship building and the maintenance of wooden hulled ships during the latter part of the eighteenth century. Vessels that were built there during that period were the *Earl of Uxbridge* (brig) 120 tons (1783); *Little John* (sloop) 13 tons (1783); *Lady Caroline* (sloop) 40 tons (1786); *Betsy* (sloop) 19 tons (1786); *Nancy* (sloop) 12 tons (1789) and *Countess of Uxbridge* (brig) 19 tons (1791).

In addition to the movement of a variety of goods by sea, the increasing exports of slates during the period 1770–1890 corresponded with a similar increase in ship-building along the north Wales coast. This provided youngsters with an alternative form of employment to that of agriculture or the slate quarries.

Rees Jones (1811-85) was born in Barmouth and, like his older brother Robert, decided to follow his father's trade and become a shipwright and builder. Having been ordained into the ministry in 1844, Rees Jones and his wife, together with their three daughters and son, William Edward, moved from Barmouth to Port Dinorwic in 1848, no doubt aware of an increasing demand for larger vessels for the slate trade. The first ship to be built by Rees Jones at Dinas was the 113 tons schooner *Palestine* launched in 1849, with Rees Jones's younger brother, John, as captain (she was lost in April 1855 off Land's End with all hands).

William Edward Jones joined his father's business in the mid-1870s and became heavily involved in the running of the ship yard. In 1875, he purchased the 1,256 tons Quebec-built ship *Dominion* (she was later mortgaged

Rees Jones, ship builder.
[W. Wyn Roberts]

to Tomkins & Platt, Bankers of Chester, possibly as a means of improving their working capital, before being sold in 1889). He was also involved with the building and subsequent management of the *Moel Eilian* and *Moel Rhiwan* for the Gwynedd Shipping Company as well as designing vessels for William Thomas of Liverpool. The Dinas shipyard, trading as Rees Jones & Son, employed between thirty and forty craftsmen, including

W.E. Jones, ship builder. [W. Wyn Roberts]

carpenters, smiths, sail-makers and labourers (due to its size the number employed increased to eighty at the time when the *Ordovic* was being built). One thirteen year old boy from Bethel who started work at Dinas as an apprentice ship's carpenter and who was involved in the building of a number of ships at the yard, including the *Ordovic*, was Robert Ffowc Williams (1852–1940). Having also served for a short period at sea as a carpenter (voyage 1889–92 to Yokohama and other far eastern ports) he was subsequently employed as a carpenter for Dinorwic Quarry at the dry dock and Gilfach Ddu, Llanberis.

Robert Ffowc Williams and his wife.
[John Fraser]

Ordovic (74874)

Of the twenty-nine vessels built at the shipyard during the second half of the nineteenth century, the 853 ton *Ordovic*, was the largest to be built in north Wales. The vessel was described as a three-masted barque with an elliptic stern, of carvel construction and measuring 168.8ft x 33.8ft x 21.3ft. Work started on the vessel on 28 March 1875.

The launching of ships at Port Dinorwic in the nineteenth century must have been a regular occurrence, but when it came to the launching of such a large vessel as the *Ordovic*, it was an event that was not going to be missed by anyone, particularly the children, as is obvious from the log-book entry by the headmaster of the local school:

2 March (1877) There was a holiday on Wednesday – the brig 'Gordovic' (correction in the margin: *Ordovic* not Gordovic) being launched. In giving the afternoon as well as morning, I have escaped the risk of having to punish in all probability about half the children for non-attendance which at present might have proved injurious [sic].

The *Cambrian News* of 9 March 1877 described the scene on the day of the launch:

The launching operations were carried on with much 'eclat', the key wedge was struck off by Mrs Wyn-Griffith, Llanfair Hall, and as soon as the blow had struck, the huge vessel made a steady start, and in a few seconds she was floating leisurely on the middle of the Menai Straits, in the care of her future conductor,

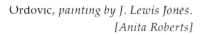

Ordovic, painting by J. Lewis Jones.
[Anita Roberts]

Form No. 19.
Signal Letters (if any)

Transcript of Register for ~~Transmission to Chief Registrar~~ of Shipping.

Official Number of Ship	Name of Ship	No., Date, and Port of Registry.
74874	"Ordovic"	4. 28th March 1877 Carnarvon

No., Date, and Port of previous Registry (if any)   new Vessel, First Registry

Whether British or Foreign Built	Whether a Sailing or Steam Ship; and if a Steam Ship, how propelled	Where Built	When Built	Name and Address of Builders
British	Sailing	Portdinorwic County of Carnarvon	1877	Rees Jones & Son Portdinorwic

				Feet	Tenths
Number of Decks	One	Length from fore part of stem, under the bowsprit, to the aft side of the head of the stern post		168	6
Number of Masts	Three				
Rigged	Barque	Main breadth to outside of plank		33	8
Stern	Elliptic	Depth in hold from tonnage deck to ceiling at midships ...		21	3
Build	Carvel				
Galleries	None	Depth in hold from upper deck to ceiling at midships, in the case of three decks and upwards			
Head	Shield				
Framework	Wood	Length of engine room, if any			

Above, below and facing: Ordovic *registration documents.* [GAS]

GROSS TONNAGE.	No. of Tons	DEDUCTIONS ALLOWED.	No. of Tons
Under Tonnage Deck	773.27	On account of space required for propelling power ...	
Closed in spaces above the Tonnage Deck, if any ...		On account of spaces occupied by Seamen or Apprentices, and appropriated to their use, and kept free from Goods or Stores of every kind, not being the personal property of the Crew	
Space or spaces between decks			
Half Poop	47.71		
Forecastle		These spaces are the following, viz. :—	
Round House		Crew Spaces	
Other closed in spaces, if any, as follows:		Deck House	10.77
Space above Half Poop	14.0	1st Mate	2.35
Deck House	17.66	2nd	1.96
		3rd Bos'n & Carpenter	1.92
	c n	Apprentices	2.42
		Cook	2.48
Gross Tonnage	852.64 2412.97	3 Reuses	1.98
Deductions, as per Contra	27.33 77.34		3.45
Registered Tonnage	825.31 2335.48	Total Deductions	27.33

Name of Master		Certificate of { Service No.
		Competency No.

Names, Residence, and Description of the Owners, and Number of Sixty-fourth Shares held by each ... } viz.,

Rees Jones of Portdinorwic, in the County of Carnarvon,   Shipbuilder _   Nineteen _ 19
William Edward Jones _   „   _   „   _   „   _   Twenty-five_ 25
Griffith Davies of Dolgelley, in the County of Merioneth , _ Watchmaker _ Two _ 2
Hugh Hughes of Tyddyn du Dolgelley _ „   _   „   _ , _ Farmer Two _ 2
Griffith Griffiths of Tyddyn y pandy, Llanbedr „ _   „   _ , _ Master Mariner. Six _ 6
William Hughes of Bodedern ?pod, Amlwch _ „ _ of Anglesea _ , _ Gentleman Five _ 5
Jane Davies, Widow } both of Bryallwyd, Menai Bridge, County of Anglesea _ (Joint-owners) _ Five _ 5
Mary Evans, Spinster }   64

Dated · 11th December 1882   the   Registrar (Signed) H G Ward

Captain Joseph Richardson (he had already served as Captain of the *Atlanta*, another of Rees Jones' ships launched in 1864).

To celebrate the successful launch, the culmination of two years' work, the builders organised a dinner for specially invited guests aboard the floating vessel before the masts and rigging had been installed. This was followed by a dinner for those who had been involved in the actual construction.

When the vessel was registered in Caernarfon on 28 March 1877, the 64-part shares were listed as being held by: Rees Jones (19/64); W.E. Jones (25/64); Griffith Davies of Dolgellau (2/64); Hugh Hughes, Dolgellau 2/64; Griffith Griffiths, Llanbedr (6/64); William Hughes, Amlwch (5/64) and Jane Davies and Mary Evans, Menai Bridge (5/64).

The day after registration, the vessel departed for her two-day voyage to Cardiff. She left there on 12 April 1877 for Java and 'other ports in the Far East'. Accompanying the forty-eight year old Captain, George Richardson, was William Roberts (mate) and Griffith Richards (2nd mate) together with David Pierce (carpenter) (1852-95) and Lewis Griffith (AB), the latter two being from Port Dinorwic. The remaining cosmopolitan crew were from a variety of countries including Malta, Copenhagen and Prussia.

Others from the village that served on the *Ordovic* during various voyages were: H. Pugh, Thomas Hughes, Robert Williams, Rees Jones Williams and John Jones. [Crew lists GAS]

Ordovic's name appears on three additional occasions in the 'Port Dinorwic shipyard ledger': 3 August 1883, 21 November and 17 March 1886, but no reason is given for such visits. However, since the vessel was still owned by W.E. Jones, the shipyard leaseholder, it is possible

David Pierce, Boston Terrace, carpenter on the Ordovic. *He died in West Africa in 1895 whilst serving aboard the RMS* Loanda. *[Nancy Pierce]*

Lady Lisgar *owned by a Port Dinorwic consortium c.1880. Robert William Owen (Halfway House Inn) served on this ship.* [Rita Bishop]

that she was there for repairs.

As a result of rising costs and the bank, Williams & Co. of Caernarfon, pressing for a loan to be repaid, the *Ordovic* was sold on 7 March 1888 for £1,600 to a John Austin of Swansea with Thomas Austin (possibly his son) taking command. The *Ordovic* left Cardiff on 14 May 1894 and was wrecked at Pasagoula some 61kms south west of the Port of Mobile, Alabama on 8 October 1894.

Rees Jones & Son ceased trading in 1897 and further evidence of continuing financial problems became apparent when W.E. Jones was issued with a County Court Summons on 2 February 1904 for the recovery of the sum of 15s 6d, being dues on a cargo of coal brought by Eliza and Mary. Four months later W.E. Jones was in arrears of dues amounting to £1 2s 7d again for a cargo of coal landed at Port Dinorwic.

The demise of ship building at Dinas may well have been hastened by two factors: wooden-hulled ships were being replaced by steel steam vessels and, as stated by a contemporary writer, W.E. Jones lacked the tact that his father possessed when dealing with the men at the shipyard.

Three other individuals living in Port Dinorwic who were greatly involved with shipping were: W.B. Buckingham, a slate agent, who lived at Nant Adda; John Millington of Bryntirion, the

The coastline along Beach Road before the reclamation of land took place, showing the Alert *high and dry until she was eventually broken up.*

Vaynol estate agent and J. Thomas Jones, a ship owner who lived at Port House. Between them they owned a considerable fleet of vessels which were involved with the slate trade as well as a number of ocean going ships. As the result of certain pressures, all the vessels had been disposed of in the 1870s and they subsequently purchased three Quebec-built ships: the *Abyssinian*, (1,265 tons) built in 1868, the *Marathon*, (1,139 tons) built in 1866 and the *Lady Lisgar*, (1,207 tons) built in 1871. They were purchased in W.B. Buckingham's name before being transferred to J.T. Jones (1816–87) as managing owner.

Ships built at Port Dinorwic by Rees Jones & Co:

Date	Name	Rig	Tonnage	
1849	Palestine	Schooner	113	lost April 1855
1850	Harriet Preston	Schooner	58	lost 1865
1853	Mary Coles	Schooner	95	lost Point Lynas
1855	John Preston	Schooner	120	lost 1882
1857	Jane Hughes	Schooner	94	lost 1859
1858	Jennett Evans	Schooner	100	sold in Ireland
1858	Menai	Schooner	96	lost 1901
1859	Margaret and Mary	Schooner	100	lost Land's End
1859	William Keith	Schooner	99	lost 1906
1860	Arvon	Schooner	100	lost 1875
1861	Ward Jackson	Schooner	97	lost near Cardiff
1861	Emily Louisa	Schooner	71	sold in Ireland
1862	Dinorwic	Schooner	124	torpedoed 1917
1862	Infanta	Schooner	45	lost off Kent
1864	Atlanta	Brigantine	223	lost 1892
1865	Vanguard	Schooner	95	sold 1874
1866	Latona	Barque	286	sold 1881
1867	Minnie Coles	Schooner	115	torpedoed 1918

Corbet's Bay c.1890.
[Len Williams]

1868	*Camelot*	Barque	345	lost
1870	*Palestine*	Brigantine	223	lost 1892
1871	*Becky Sharp*	Smack	40	lost 1876
1871	*Maggie Woodburne*	Schooner	108	fate unknown
1873	*A.M. Rowlands*	Brigantine	176	sold in Amlwch
1877	*Ordovic*	Barque	860	lost Pasagoula, USA
1878	*Velinheli*	Schooner	65	sold 1909
1880	*Miss Williams*	Schooner	79	lost 1906
1886	*Ruby*	Ketch	44	sold
1895	*E.E. Muspratt*	Ketch	80	sold in Liverpool
1897	*Empress Climax*	Ketch	80	beached locally

Schooner: vessel with fore and aft sails on two or more masts or with top and topgallant sails.
Ketch: two-masted coasting vessel.
Brigantine: two-masted vessel with the main mast of a schooner and the foremast of a brigantine.
Barque: three-masted ship of a particular rig.
Smack: small-decked or half-decked coaster rigged as cutter, sloop or yawl.

Other ships mentioned in a ledger relating to ship-building in the yard:

1882 schooner *Boadicea* – Capt. Francis
1882 smack *Barbara Elizabeth*
1882 schooner *Bessie Rowe*
1883 schooner of Caernarvon *Barbara*
1886 schooner *Britannia* – Capt. Hugh Jones
1882 schooner *Climax* – Capt. Richard Jones
1882 schooner *Catherine Roberts* – Capt. Griffith Williams
1883 schooner *Cambria* – Capt. John Williams
1884 schooner – Capt. John Hughes of Amlwch
1884 schooner *Crystal Spring* – Capt. Richard Edwards
1882 schooner *Dinorwic* – Capt. John Elias
1882 schooner *Emily Louisa* – Capt. William Jones
1883 schooner *Galloway Lass* – Capt. Roberts
1897 PS *America* was brought to Dinas to be scrapped. She may well have been the last vessel to be 'dealt with' at the shipyard.

[GAS XM4622/1, 2, DQ3601]

Old shipbuilding yard at Dinas
A document referring to renting the yard and workshop at an annual cost of £15, stated 'The slip cradle is much out of repair and £150 would be required to put it in order. The trade in shipping has departed and no doubt a future lessee must look for other means of support such as yacht and boat building'. [GAS XD35/71]

The old yard remained unused until Mr H.G. Crossfield, a Warrington soap manufacturer, decided to build yachts as a 'hobby or a side-line' at the near derelict yard. The work was to be undertaken by boat builders J.R. Foulkes & Co. The newly-established enterprise was managed by Joseph Alfred Foulkes and John Roberts was appointed foreman of the yard. Many of the carpenters, including Thomas Evans (Florence House), previously employed at the old yard, were re-engaged. The first Gunter-rigged

The old shipyard and workshops at Dinas with W.E. Parker's cruiser on the slipway. [F. Statham]

yacht to be built was the *Mayflower* (24 tons displacement), followed by *Sweet Brier*, a wooden sloop of 31ft overall and 5ft draft and having a petrol engine.

Captain Richard Thomas Foulkes, the son of J.R. Foulkes, died August 1919, and a report in a local paper stated:

> On Sunday night, after a brief illness, the death occurred of Captain Richard Foulkes, of The House-Boat, Dinas, at the advanced age of 84. He was a native of Flintshire, but had resided in this neighbourhood for the last ten years. He leaves four sons and three daughters. The funeral took place on Thursday morning, at Llanfairisgaer Churchyard. The service was conducted by the Rev. J.T. Jones (vicar of the parish). [C&DH 8 August 1919]

Although Capt. Richard Foulkes lived, as stated in the obituary, on a houseboat at Dinas whilst the yachts were being built, other members of Foulkes family were at Porth Edwen, Anglesey. It

Captain Richard Thomas Foulkes. [Glyn Foulkes]

The houseboat used by Richard Thomas Foulkes. [Glyn Foulkes]

The Foulkes family at Dinas. [Glyn Foulkes]

is believed that the family's connection with Port Dinorwic and Anglesey continued until *circa* 1928.

Mr and Mrs W.E. Parker, Dinas, Port Dinorwic

William Eaton Parker was born at Liverpool, the son of wealthy parents who had cotton mills in Manchester. He decided at a young age that he wanted to see something of the world and consequently spent time in America, India and China, experiencing many escapades on the way. No doubt attracted to north Wales, and to the Menai Strait in particular, by his love of the sea, he and his wife became involved with Dinas in 1909 a short while after their youngest daughter was born (yacht building at Dinas was well established by this time). A document dated 1910 referring to the 'main building' stated:

> Mr Parker pays Mr Foulkes £6 for the house and Mr Foulkes pays Mr W.E. Jones £26 pa, half rates paid by Mr Parker … there are 2 or 3 sheds that have absolutely gone beyond repair – one is a mere skeleton … The partition in the dwelling house was put up by Mr Foulkes. The place is altogether very untied and would look better if clear of debris … office, ship carpenter's shed and loft and Dwelling House, saw pit and boat shed. Building not safe – props rotten …

A further letter that year stated

… visited this place [Dinas shore] in the evening of Tuesday 14 June with Mr James Owen. Saw Mr J.R. Foulkes who said that he had arranged with Messrs Jones to take over the lease and that it was his intention to wall in the ground for the purpose of carrying on his trade of ship and boat repairing … Foulkes paid W.E. Jones £30 for the Patent slip 3 years ago …

The Mayflower *built at Dinas.*
[Glyn Foulkes]

Until the debris referred to had been cleared Mr Parker and the family lived in the old workshop alongside the slipway. When writing to her family in 1909 she described the sad state of the old ship-building yard:

> There are 2 or 3 sheds that have absolutely gone beyond repair ... The place is altogether very untidy and would look better if clear of debris ... office, ship carpenter's shed and loft and Dwelling House, sawpit and boat shed. Building not safe – props rotten.

W.E. Parker's house c.1910. The extension at the back was built for his daughter, Dorothy, and son-in-law, Richard Barrington, who was involved with the Marconi radio station at Waenfawr. [Vernon Bowles]

In another letter Mrs Parker, who referred to her husband as 'Eaton', vividly describes daily life at Dinas to her mother:

> 13 December 1909 I could not give you any idea what the house is like but it can be made very nice with a little trouble and work. Just now it looks from outside (very cosy in) like a sort of coachman's house over stables or something of that sort, it is just a part of the sheds partitioned off with an old steamers staircase to go up to the only door that we have. Looks the funniest little place you ever saw outside but inside it is really very cosy except when we have an easterly wind like today and we cannot get warm, being all an open shed under us facing this wind it nearly blows us off our feet through the cracks in the floor but we are all very well are not really far from the shops just a nice walk and I manage to get once a week somehow but we are better off in that respect than usual as a great many carts come around Milk, Paraffin, Veg, etc, all come to the door and they are fishing all the time just opposite.

Mr Parker, possibly with assistance from the Foulkes family, not only built a house on the transformed site but also developed a large walled garden where he had a small collection of animals including bears, an alligator and snakes, as well as domestic animals. When the bears became large and difficult to handle, they were given to Chester Zoo.

In 1940, Harry L. Dowsett bought control of Brooke Marine Ltd at Lowestoft and subsequently leased the old boatyard at Dinas as a shadow facility, scrapping the old slipway and workshops and building large sheds on the site. In 1943, the company became Dowsett MacKay (Dow-Mac) and in May of that year, the Admiralty placed an order for various tug and barge prototypes, which were to be pre-fabricated in Lowestoft before being brought by rail to Port Dinorwic for assembly. Specialist workers were brought to Port Dinorwic by the parent company while the unskilled men were recruited locally. Eventually, the contract was for 500 vessels which were to be all riveted, flat-bottomed tugs. Some were approximately 55ft in length, powered by twin-screw petrol engines with an open wheelhouse aft, whilst others were to be five feet shorter and

Above left: The nearness to William Parker's home to the Dow-Mac barge-building yard is apparent from this photograph. [Brooke Marine archive]

Above right: Barge in the course of construction alongside the original shipyard workshop. [Brooke Marine archive]

Right: A Brooke Marine tug. The pathway in the background passed beneath the mainline railway and on to the main road. (Brooke Marine archive]

The Brooke Marine sheds that replaced the old workshops. [Len Williams]

powered by a single-screw petrol engine. These were prefabricated, assembled and dismantled into kit form (for reassembly in the Far East in support of military operations against Japan). However, the sudden end of the war in the Far East found a large number of these Unicraft vessels surplus to requirements. According to Alec Dancer, a foreman at the yard noted:

> Some 500 … craft [were] been left over from the war effort. Harry Dowsett … knew there was a market for those types of craft on the rivers of the African countries with a peanut scheme. After two years nearly all had been completed and sent out as deck cargo to African countries.

We also had a contract to repair RAF rescue high-speed craft that were stationed at Menai Bridge.

An agreement dated 27 July 1943 between Dowsett MacKay and William Eaton Parker indicated that the latter was employed (at a wage of £2 10s 0d per week) to act as a consultant in matters relating to local conditions such as river currents, supply of labour and materials. The agreement was to run for a period of five years, unless otherwise decided by the company. Doubtless, the agreement may well have been an appeasement and token compensation for the loss of peace and tranquillity that had drawn the Parker family to Dinas. The incessant noise and dirt that they had to suffer must have been virtually unbearable. William Eaton Parker died on 19 January 1951 at the age of eighty-one and his wife on 19 April 1968, aged ninety.

APPENDIX 1
LOCAL SHIPS AND MARINERS

Dinorwic (44234) (1862–1917)
The three-masted 99 ton wooden schooner measuring 80ft 3ins x 22ft x 11ft 5ins was built in 1862 by Rees Jones & Son at Dinas, Port Dinorwic. She was owned by Robert Griffith, 10 Chapel Street, Caernarfon and her master was Capt. J.O. Griffiths. Amongst the crew were William Cale and John Pritchard, both of whom were from Bangor and had served on the *Elizabeth Bennett*. *Dinorwic* was scuttled ten nautical miles south of Hastings by the submarine UB-40 on 15 July 1917. The crew survived.

Elizabeth (12386)
The 37 ton *Elizabeth*, registered in 1856, carried a variety of cargoes including slate. The owner and master in 1864 was Richard Owen, Nefyn. Forty years later, she was owned and captained by John Huxley Hughes, 50 Chapel Street, Caernarfon with a crew that included Owen Huxley who was later to serve on the *Virtue*.

Arvon (28541) (1863–99)
The *Arvon* was owned by Capt. Owen Owens, Halfway House, Port Dinorwic from 1872 until 1892 when he sold her to Capt. W. Parry, 15 Castle Street, Caernarfon. When Captain Owens was not on board as master, the vessel would be under the control of Capt. William Parry with Frances Jones as mate and Theophilus Jones and Robert Ellis as able seamen.

Sarah (1501) (1871–79)
Of 52 tons and registered at Caernarfon in 1871. The crew list for 1879 gives the owner as Robert Owen and master as David Pugh. Whilst sailing between Holyhead and Runcorn in October 1879 that year she was wrecked on Rhyl beach.

Sarah (10192) (1854–73)
This 23-ton vessel was used primarily for carrying stone between Caernarfon and Port Dinorwic.

James (10278)
The men that served on this 58-ton schooner were mostly from Port Dinorwic and Caernarfon and included: 1872 – Owen Huxley; 1892 – John Jones, 3 Menai Street, Port Dinorwic, John Roberts; 1896 – William Evans, Andrew Maguire; 1899 – Charles Bowles; 1903 – Jeremiah Davies;

1904 – Capt. John Huxley Hughes; 1911 – Thomas Lillie, Owen John Elias, Hugh Roberts, Peter Dop, Jenkin Thomas Williams, John Davies, Owen Richard Williams; 1912 – Robert James Bowles, Hugh David Parry, John Dop and Hugh Dop.

Virtue (70313) (1876–1913)

In 1882, this 16-ton smack was owned by Henry Hughes and the master was Owen Huxley. After being employed as a carpenter during the construction of the Britannia Bridge, John Pierce Jones (1825–1907), a native of Llanfair PG, came to work as a carpenter on ships being built at Dinas and by 1913 (when he was living at Frondeg, Port Dinorwic) he had taken her over as both owner and master with John Pierce Jones, also of Port Dinorwic, as mate. He was also the owner of three other small ships, namely the *Royal Charter*, *Neptune* and *Harmony*. During the second half of the nineteenth century, when there was much building work being carried out at Port Dinorwic, the *Virtue* was mostly used to transport sand from Chwarel Goch in Anglesey. She also carried a variety of cargoes between Caernarfon, Porthdinllaen, Port Dinorwic, Beaumaris, Trefor, Parkia Brick Works and Lewis Wharf (Bangor).

Velinheli (80227) (1878–1909)

The first vessel to be named *Velinheli* was a two-masted schooner of 75 tons, carvel built and with an elliptic stern. Built in Port Dinorwic by Rees Jones & Co., she measured 75ft x 21ft x 10ft and was registered at Caernarfon on 21 October 1878. Between 1878 and 1909, she was owned and managed by John Dean a slate merchant of Blackburn. Her first master was fifty-one year old G. Williams of 3 Bodlondeb Terrace, Port Dinorwic whose crew included: mate – John Jones and able seamen – John Thomas and Rowland Pritchard. By 1888, Griffith Griffiths had taken over as master, followed by Thomas M. Williams in 1890 and James Hollingworth in 1891. She was sold on 27 May 1891 to Arthur Evans, a coal merchant, of Greystones, County Wicklow, Ireland for £850, the transaction being registered at the Custom House, Caernarfon. *Velinheli* was eventually lost after a collision with the Blue Funnel ship *Laertes* of Liverpool in fog in Liverpool Bay on 25 January 1915 but happily the crew of four, Capt. Hollensworth, Mr Byrne, Mr Cleary and Mr Hunt were rescued as was the cat.

Mary B. Mitchell (97575)

Built at the shipyard of Paul Rogers & Co., of Carrickfergus in Northern Ireland, this 227-ton three-masted, steel-hulled, topsail schooner measuring 129ft x 24ft x 11ft was registered at Beaumaris. Following her launch on 30 March 1892, she was towed by the steamer *Anglesey* to Port Penrhyn. The very high standard of fittings throughout the vessel, the accommodation for both officers and men and the fact that she could sail without ballast, gave her the appearance of being more suitable for private use rather than as a slate carrier.

According to the ship's agreement of 30 June 1893, the master was Capt. J. Jones of Port Dinorwic and the mate Griffith Rees. Rees's wife Ann (1837–1930) who not only raised a family and was a midwife in Port Dinorwic, but also found time to sign on occasionally as a cook to sail with her husband. The *Mary B. Mitchell* carried Dinorwic and Penrhyn slates from Port Dinorwic to Aberdeen and other Scottish ports, Ireland and London.

While bound for Hamburg with slate, she went aground on the Texal Bank, Holland on 27 December 1896 and was badly damaged and sank. She was re-floated on the 18 January 1897 and repaired before being sold in 1898 to E.A. Young. She was involved in a further accident while anchored in Weymouth Roads on 31 January 1903 when she lost her bowsprit and her stern was damaged when struck by the cruiser HMS *Hogue*. During the First World War, the *Mary B. Mitchell* was requisitioned by the Admiralty and used as a Q-ship under the command of Lieutenant M. Armstrong, RNR. Armed with one 12-pounder and two 6-pounder guns, together with two Lewis guns, she sailed under a variety of names including *Mitchell, Q9* and *Mary y José*. As the result of a gale, she was driven ashore on 15 December 1944 at Torrs Point near Kirkcudbright and wrecked. Once again the crew of eight were saved. [UWB BP 37089, 97575]

Polly Preston (47753)

Polly Preston, a schooner of 98 tons and measuring 89ft 6ins x 22ft 6ins x 11ft 7 ins, was registered at Caernarfon in 1863. She was owned by Robert Preston and her master was Capt. Evan Davies. She carried on average a crew of nine men. By June 1887, ownership had transferred to L. Williams & Son, Florence Terrace, Port Dinorwic and the master was Capt. David Williams of Port Dinorwic. The following year, Lewis Williams continued as owner but his son Capt. Robert Williams had been appointed as master. By 1898 (and for the next four years), the owner was shown as Hugh Owen, Cefn Farm, Port Dinorwic and the master as Capt. Robert Williams.

For the independently owned vessels to ensure profitability, it was essential that their period in dock awaiting a cargo was as short as possible. Equally as important was that after a delivery had been made, she returned with a cargo rather than in ballast. With an increasing number of ships arriving at Port Dinorwic in the latter half of the nineteenth century to be loaded with slate, a method had to be devised as to the order of loading. The captains met outside the quay office at 11 a.m. each morning to discuss the allocation of cargoes to ships depending on the weight involved and the intended destination.

To meet an increasing demand for slate and a faster and more efficient method of delivery G.W.D. Assheton Smith decided to purchase steamships. The main commodity being exported from Port Dinorwic during the eighteenth and nineteenth centuries and the early part of the twentieth century was slate which was both heavy to load onto the ship and store in the hold. Despite this, it could easily be damaged if heavy weather was encountered on a voyage. For this reason, the Dinorwic Quarry steamships, in particular the *Vaynol*, *Velinheli*, *Enid* and *Elidir* were specially designed to carry slate. The *Elidir*, the largest of the three and considered to be capable of withstanding the harshest weather, would undertake the longer voyages (and possibly the most difficult) to Lerwick in the Shetland Isles, Wick, Aberdeen, Peterhead and Frazerburgh. After delivering a cargo of slate, she would occasionally return with a ballast of granite from Aberdeen which would be discarded onto the dockside at Port Dinorwic prior to loading its next consignment of slate. This granite was used in the construction of a number of houses in the village, including Frondeg Terrace (later renamed as Terfyn Terrace). Depending on the distance involved and the weather encountered on a voyage, the four steam ships would aim to undertake an average of two voyages a week.

SS *Dinorwic* (92205) (1892–1919)

The *Dinorwic* was the first of the Dinorwic Quarry steam ships was built by S. McKnight & Co. of Ayr in 1892. She was of 276 tons and measured 128ft x 23ft x 10ft 4ins. Having arrived on 19 January 1892, within two days she sailed for Kirkaldy with a cargo of slate. She had a two-cylinder compound engine built by William Kemp of Glasgow. The owner's name was given as the Hon. W.W. Vivian, Plas Dinorwic, who managed the estate on behalf of Assheton Smith. The master of the vessel was Thomas Williams and the crew consisted of: Thomas John Jones, John Roberts, Andrew Maguire, William Caddock, Thomas Wilson and Evan Hughes (who had previously served on the first *Velinheli*). Other crew members listed over the years, some of whom become master mariners, were Daniel Davies, John Roberts, Owen Donaldson, Llewelyn Pritchard, William Jones, Robert Pierce, William Evans, Edward M. Williams, Richard Pritchard, John Jones, Owen J. Elias, Owen Jones and Hugh G. Owens. Typically, the voyages undertaken by the *Dinorwic* transporting slate from Port Dinorwic were to Middlesbrough, Dublin, Boston (Lincolnshire), Hull and Newcastle. In addition, she inaugurated a delivery of slate to London, the first of eight visits that she made to the capital. The *Dinorwic* was sold in 1919.

SS Dinorwic.
*Note the Dinorwic
Quarries intertwined
DQ on the funnel.
[Emyr Wyn Roberts]*

SS *Vaynol* (92210) 1892–1902

The company's second steamship was the 233-ton *Vaynol* which measured 129ft x 22ft x 7ft 7ins. She too was built in 1892 by S. McKnight & Co. arriving in Port Dinorwic on 22 December. Within two days, she was loaded with slate and sailed for Siloth in Cumberland. Her two-cylinder compound engine was built by Muir & Houston, Glasgow. She was in service for a period of ten years before sinking in the Mull of Galloway following a collision with the steam trawler *Lucerne*. Amongst those who served on her were John Jones, Thomas Jones, William Evans, William Jones and Thomas Hughes (the latter three also served on the SS *Dinorwic*).

SS Vaynol *at Port Dinorwic. [Viv Smith]*

SS *Velinheli* (102641) 1892–1941

The last of the trio to be purchased by Assheton Smith was the 125-ton *Velinheli*, built by S. McKnight & Co. She arrived in Port Dinorwic on 5 March 1892 but, during the following nine days, whilst still in the dock, was loaded and unloaded twice, possibly due to a disagreement over her carrying capacity. She was returned to Ayr and subsequently sold as the *Dunlossit*. She was eventually repurchased by the Dinorwic Quarry in 1894 and her name reverted to *Velinheli*. Measuring 95ft x 18ft 5ins x 7ft 5ins, she was the smallest purpose-built, slate-carrying vessel owned by the Dinorwic Quarry. Capable of delivering 49 tons on each trip, her 40hp compound engine enabled her to attain a speed of $9^1/2$ knots. Accommodation was provided for the captain, mate and two engineers beneath the bridge, whilst two seamen and two firemen shared the forecastle. The fore and aft sails appear to be a relic of days before steam, although it was said that

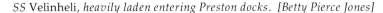

SS Velinheli, *heavily laden entering Preston docks. [Betty Pierce Jones]*

they were useful under suitable weather conditions provided the captain had had previous experience under canvas. Due to her small size, it was not unusual for the *Velinheli* to arrive, be loaded and then depart on the same tide. Such a turnaround was good from a business point of view, but it was very stressful for the captain in particular, and to a lesser degree, the crew. Immediately after the ship had docked, there would be a rush to get home for clean clothes and fresh food which the captain and crew were responsible for. Although ships' crews were allowed double rations during the Second World War (when compared to the civilian population), replenishing their food store within the time allowed ashore was always a problem. The storing of food on board ship was also difficult since refrigeration was unavailable. Even when stored in a cupboard inaccessible to mice and rats, it tended to deteriorate quickly particularly during the summer months.

Amongst those who served on her were: J.H. Jones, Thomas Wilson Roberts, T.E. Hughes, Robert Pierce, William Evans, Thomas Pritchard, Isaac Jones, Thomas Jones, William Jones, Robert Caddock, William Caddock, Ellis Edwards and Owen Roberts. During her forty-seven years of delivering slate the ports that she most frequently visited were: Dublin, Preston, Belfast, Birkenhead, Runcorn and Liverpool where she would often transfer her cargo to ocean-going vessels. She was sold in 1941.

SS *Enid* (118501) 1903–54

SS *Enid*, 267 tons, built by Ailsa Shipbuilding Co. in 1903. She measured 131ft 5ins x 22ft 3 ins x 7ft 8 ins and her engine, built by Ross & Duncan of Glasgow, enabled her to attain a speed of nine knots. Her crew over a number of years included: Daniel Davies, John Davies, Griffith Evans, William Evans (previously with the SS *Dinorwic*), E. Hughes, Thomas Hughes (previously with the SS *Dinorwic*), John Jones, Thomas Jones (previously with the SS *Vaynol*), William Jones (previously with the SS *Velinheli*), John Lewis (previously with the SS *St Tudwal*), Andrew Maguire (previously with the SS *Alistair*), Robert Pierce, William Pierce (previously with the SS *Dinorwic*), Owen Pritchard, Edward Roberts, John Roberts (previously with the SY *Marguerite*) and Richard Williams.

SS Enid.
[William Hughes]

During the Second World War, instructions were received in August 1942 that certain alterations to the vessel had to be carried out. These included the fitting of '… plastic armour around the wheelhouse and both wings of bridge to be extended in order that twin Lewis guns could be fitted.' Her armaments also included an Oerlikon gun, but there is no record of the crew having to make use of the weapons. The ammunition that she carried consisted of '400 cartridges SA 20 mm Oerlikon HE, 180 practice, 180 tracer – 200 rounds .303 rifle.' In addition, a liferaft complete with all equipment, capable of carrying twelve people, had to be provided together with 'provisions consisting of hand rockets, rustproof drinking vessels, waterproof bags, 24 x 1lb tins of sweet, condensed milk'.

In November 1945, O.T. Williams, the Dinorwic Quarry general manager, wrote to the Admiralty stating that the alarm bells and Marconi emergency wireless transmitter were being removed from the *Enid* and asking for instructions as to where they should be sent as they (the company) had no further use for them on the vessel.

Having given fifty-one years' service, she was placed for sale with Thomas McLaren & Co. of Glasgow for £7,500 and eventually sold for scrap to the Hammond Lane Metal Company of Dublin.

SS *Elidir* (118502) 1903–42

The 423-ton SS *Elidir* was built in 1903 at S. McKnight & Co. (later known as Ailsa Shipbuilding Co.) for G.W.D. Assheton Smith. She measured 151ft 6ins x 25ft 1ins x 9ft 9 ins and, when weather allowed, would undertake the longest voyages from Port Dinorwic round the north of Scotland to Aberdeen and Wick. Her three-cylinder engine was built by Ross & Duncan of Glasgow. The first master to serve on her was Capt. Thomas Williams with Thomas Wilson Roberts as mate. Other members of the crew at various times were: Charles Bowles, A. Doyle, Hugh Evans, Griffith Jones, John T. Jones, William Jones, Andrew Maguire, John Owen, Henry R. Pierce, John Roberts, Robert D. Vaughan, Edward Martin Williams and Owen Williams.

Although Thomas Wilson Roberts is shown as being the master in 1906, it was Capt. Thomas Williams who handed over command of the *Elidir* to Capt. William Evans on 12 October 1909. His crew in 1910 included Edward Martin Williams, Hugh Pritchard, Thomas J. Williams, Johnnie Hughes, Richard Pritchard, Andrew Maguire, Griffith Jones, Daniel Davies, John Roberts (who

SS Elidir.
[William Hughes]

had previously been with the SY *Amalthea*) and Owen Donaldson (previously with the SS *Dinorwic*). The following report was made by the captain in the ship's log for 19 October 1913: 'At 11.30 a.m. found Andrew Maguire second engineer in his bed dead, my attention drawn to this occurrence by Griffith Jones, fireman. I at once sent for the police who came on board at midday and removed the body to the mortary [sic] inquest was held today 20 inst – balance of wages due £2 1s 0d'. Andrew Maguire (1863–1913), who was born at Penrhyn, Cornwall, had worked on a number of the Vaynol ships including the SS *Vaynol*. He joined the SS *Elidir* in 1904 as leading fireman before becoming second engineer nine years later.

Apart from the Dinorwic Quarry ships: *Enid*, *Elidir* and *Velinheli*, the only other vessels recorded as being involved in the carriage of slate during the period of the First World War were the *Tern* (Capt. Morris) and *Duke of York* (Capt. Plumpton).

After serving as mate, Owen J. Jones took command of the *Elidir* in 1933. Two of his crew members were Griffith Evans as chief engineer and Goronwy Owen as fireman. Due to the general slump in trade during the 1930s, which also affected the slate industry, it was necessary for ships like the *Elidir* to look elsewhere for cargoes. As a result, she would spend up to six months at a time on the east coast of England carrying coal to London and returning with iron ore, only returning to Port Dinorwic when she was due for routine maintenance such as boiler cleaning.

By 1942, the small quantity of slate being produced under wartime conditions could either be carried by rail or road without resorting to the obvious dangers of sailing. Consequently, Capt. Jones's last cargo was a load of salt from Runcorn to Glasgow, returning to Connah's Quay in ballast. When he retired from the sea, Capt. Jones was appointed as harbour master at Port Dinorwic.

As the result of the Coppack Brothers ship *Farfield* being sunk by a German aircraft off Bardsey Island in 1941, the company purchased the *Elidir* from the Dinorwic Quarry in 1942. After being requisitioned by the Admiralty, her main mast was moved forward and her main hatch lengthened. Alterations were also carried out to the crews quarters in Liverpool in November 1942 at a cost of £661 19s 6d. In addition, rolling chocks were fitted in August 1943 to improve stability at a cost of £544 13s 4d. She was in service between 30 November 1943 and May 1944 with the admiralty in what was described as 'Miscellaneous Military' which initially meant being used for commando training

At the time of the D-Day landings in Normandy, the *Elidir* sailed as part of 'Convoy ETC3W 9th', from the Thames via the Solent to the Gold sector of the Normandy beaches. She also took supplies across the channel and landed them at the Mulberry Harbour in Normandy and in Dieppe, Ostend and Caen before eventually returning to Southampton. During this period, the *Elidir* was under the command of either Capt. Edward A. Bennett or Capt. B.J. Bennett. Other members of the crew were: mate (also described as bosun) – F.S. Bennett or J.V. Prince; chief engineer – Arthur Bennett, Griffith Evans or B. Evans; 2nd Engineer – Walter Palmer or Goronwy Owen; AB – A. Yates; Firemen – W. Jellicoe, Thomas P. Owen, A. Farrigia, Eric Williams and Goronwy Owen; OS – V. Spark. She also carried two gunners. As an example of the rate of pay

SS Harlow Plain.

at this time, Walter Palmer as second engineer received £1 for eight hours work or £7 19s 10d for the week. Correspondence between Coppack and the Ministry of War Transport relating to the requisitioning continued until January 1946. Four members of the crew who were from Port Dinorwic at the time when she was involved in the D-Day landings were: Griffith Evans, Thomas P. Owen, Walter Palmer and Eric Williams. The *Elidir* was broken up for scrap in 1955. [FRO Coppack Bros, Connah's Quay – D/CK/281 and 282]

SS *Harlow Plain* (462/21)
The *Harlow Plain* was built by J. Lewis & Son in Aberdeen in 1921. Capt. Ben Williams (1876–1952) was in command from 1921 to 1931 and her crew consisted of Richard Dop, William Favretto, Walter Horlock, Robert David Howard, John Jones and Richard Thomas. A typical voyage for the vessel was to take a cargo of slate from Port Dinorwic to Aberdeen, then coal to Ireland. She was sold to a company in France and renamed *Cherbourg*.

SS *Veronica Tennant* (1928–54)
The *Veronica Tennant* was launched in 1922 for Frederick Horlock as *Ipswich Trader* but not completed as the builders Colby Brothers of Lowestoft ceased trading. In 1928, she was completed by the Mistley Shipbuilding & Repair Company and in 1935 lengthened by 20ft. She was purchased by Duff, Herbert & Mitchell Ltd (representing the Dinorwic Quarry) in 1946 and renamed *Veronica Tennant*. She was broken up at Llanelli in 1954.

After the Second World War, the Dinorwic Quarry Company purchased a number of second-hand coasters, including the *Dawlish*, *Alfred Mason*, *Sybil Mary* and *Juliet Duff*. Although the latter was managed by O.T. Williams, who had charge of all the quarry ships, she was registered in the name of Duff, Herbert & Mitchell Ltd and carried their colours. This arrangement continued until the dispatch of slate was taken over either by rail or by road.

Local Mariners

The following list is not definitive. The figure displayed after the date of death is the age at death:

Capt. Joseph Acton, *ob.* 14.07.1862, 53

Capt. Thomas Maurice Acton, *ob.* 24.01.1888, 54

Engineer Charles James Bowles, MN, Second World War

PO Charles Henry Butler, *ob.* during the First World War

William Caddock, 73 Bangor Street

Chief Officer John Cecil Chubb

Sidney Mons Chubb, MN, *ob.* 10.10.1942, 27

Daniel Davies, 3 Moelydon Terrace

Capt. John Davies, Frondirion, MN, 26.10.1893, 61

John Davies, MN, Second World War

Capt. J.W. Davies, *ob.* 1939, 69

Capt. Lewis Davies, *Harriette Preston*, died.01.1883, 44

Robert Davies, Harbour Master, *ob.* 17.03.1915, 62

Chief Officer Peter Dop, *Linda Blanche*, Second World War

Captain Robert Dop, MV *St Tudno*

Capt. Richard Edwards, Wern, Llanfairisgaer, *ob.* 26.07.1900, 61

Robert Edwards, *ob.* 16.08.1856, 48

Thomas Edwards, *ob.* 1.03.1867, 26

William Edwards, Trinity Pilot, *ob.* 21.06.1904, 65

Capt. John Elias, 1 Port Terrace, *ob.* 3.10.1889, 63

Capt. Owen Elias, Bodawain, *ob.* 25.01.1924, 74

William Morris Elias, 1 Port Terrace

Capt. Henry Ellis, *ob.* 26.04.1880, 72

John Ellis, Menai Street, *Annie*, *ob.* 27.10.1892

Capt. John Ellis, *ob.* 19.04.1899, 48

PO John Ellis, Bryn Melyn, RNVR, First World War

Capt. John Ellis, 41 Bangor Street, 1919

Chief Officer William Ellis, MN, *ob.* 1942, 41

Griffith Evans, 19 Snowdon Street, engineer serving 45 years at sea

Capt. Henry Evans, Boston Street, *Annie*, *ob.* 27.10.1892

Robert Evans, 28 Beach Row, *Bodecia*, *ob.* 5.03.1890, 22

Thomas Evans, *ob.* 31.05.1866, 57

Capt. William Evans, 11 Port Terrace, *ob.* 4.03.1925, 93

Capt. William Evans, SS *Elidir*, *ob.* 19.08.1951, 85;

Chief Officer, William Favretto, MN, Second World War

Capt. Henry Francis, 9 Port Terrace, *ob.* 5.03.1890

Capt. Alex Grant, Pen-y-Wern, *ob.* 3.02.1924, 80

John Griffiths, *ob.* 1.06.1865, 55

Llewellyn Griffith, RN, Tan-y-Maes, First World War

Capt. William Evans. [Kathleen W. Roberts]

Capt. Owen Griffiths, *ob.* 21.05.1896, 77

William Hatton, 6 Menai Street

Richard Hayward, *ob.* 6.09.1885, 19

Walter W. Horlock, 60 Bangor Street

Edward Hughes

Chief Officer Herbert Ellis Hughes, MN, Second World War

Capt. Hugh Hughes, 6 Sea View Terrace, *ob.* 1901

John Hughes, 6 Helen Terrace, RN, First World War

Richard Hughes, MN, Second World War

Capt. William Hughes, Bangor Street, SS *Penrhyn*, *ob.* 1953

William Humphreys, Augusta Place, *ob.* 24.08.1935, 78

Capt. David Jones, Menai Hill, *ob.* 5.05.1874, 75

PO David Jones, RNR, First World War

Ellis Jones, sailor, Snowdon Street, *ob.* 21.06.1884, 65

Capt. Evan Jones, Gorphwysfa, *ob.* 1882, 65

Francis Jones, Aber Cottage, *ob.* 24.07.1867, 25

Griffith Jones, 9 Menai Street, *ob.* 5.01.1932, 67

Capt. Griffith Jones, 2 Bangor Street, *ob.* 1884, 54

Capt. Griffith Jones, Bodafon, died.11.1945

Henry Jones, *Alice Davies*, *ob.* 21.11.1878, 17

Henry Jones, Beach Road, *Restless*, *ob.* 23.08.1895

Capt. Henry Jones, Awelfryn, *ob.* 10.10.1933, 74

Capt. Hugh Jones, 13 Menai Street, *ob.* 16.09.1913, 83

John Jones, 1 Augusta Place

John Jones, Glanhwfa, *ob.* 19.02.1907, 37

Chief Officer John Jones, *ob.* 1885

Capt. John Jones, Mona House, *Bessie Rowe*, *ob.* 3.08.1878, 57

Capt. John Jones, The Moorings, *ob.* 11.10.1911, 43

Capt. John Jones, Menai Street, SS *Enid*, *ob.* 2.11.1926, 79

Capt. J. Jones, Minnie Coles

Capt. J. Jones, Bush Road

J.D. Jones, Port Cottage, SS *Englishman*

Capt. John Hughes Jones, 12 Menai Street, *ob.* 15.10.1924, 72

John Morris Jones, MN, Second World War

Capt. John T. Jones, Menai Street, *ob.* 14.04.1894, 28

John Theophilus Jones, 19 Beach Road

Capt. Owen Jones, Alun Terrace, *ob.* 16.11.1885, 55

Capt. Owen John Jones, Y Dderwen, *ob.* 16.07.1974

Capt. R. Jones, *Fairy*

Capt. Richard Jones, *ob.* 18.05.1865, 52

Capt. Richard Jones, Bryn Goleu, *ob.* 19.01.1909, 72;

Robert Jones, *ob.* 16.01.1886, 73

Capt. R.E. Jones, Cartref, Bangor, *ob.* 6.03.1929

Capt. R.O. Jones, The Cliff

R.W. Jones, Augusta Place, SS *George*, *ob.* 29.01.1907, 30

Walter W. Horlock and grandson.

Lewis Owen.
[John Bryan Owen]

Capt. Owen Owens.
[Yvonne Roberts]

Walter Palmer. [Bruce Palmer]

Capt. Theophilus Jones, Snowdon Street, *Venerable*, *ob.* 1888, 52
Capt. Thomas S. Jones, Sea View Terrace, *ob.* 16.10.1885, 60
William Jones, *ob.* 9.03.1840, 52
Capt. W. Jones, Bronfa, Bangor Street
Capt. William Jones, Frondeg Terrace, *ob.* 1869, 52
Capt. William Jones, *Commodore*, *ob.* 11.03.1890, 90
Capt. William Jones, *Emily Louisa*, *ob.* 7.04.1890, 44
Capt. William Jones, *ob.* 3.12.1910, 48
Capt. William Jones, Velinheli Terrace, SS *Dinorwic*, *ob.* 14.02.1915, 43
William Jones, Snowdon Street, *ob.* 10.03.1915, 40
Capt. William Jones, Bodlondeb, *ob.* 1963
William Richard Jones, MN, First World War
Capt. W.R. Jones, Bodwyn, *ob.* 1933
Capt. David Lewis, 11 Port Terrace, *ob.* 21.03.1884, 65
Capt. Lewis Lewis, Glanhwfa, *ob.* 14.01.1931, 73
Capt. Thomas Lillie, *ob.* 16.06.1949, 83
Andrew Maguire, 21 Snowdon Street, SS *Elidir*, *ob.* 19.10.1913, 50
Richard Maguire, 21 Snowdon Street, *ob.* 15.07.1942, 34
William Richard Maguire, MN, Second World War
Donald Mackay, *ob.* 1.06.1865, 55
Griffith Morgan, Menai Street, *Annie*, *ob.* 27.10.1892, 21
John Morris, SS *Arandora Star*, *ob.* 1.07.1940, 49
David Owen, *ob.* 29.01.1868, 55
Emlyn Owen, AB, MN, Second World War
Goronwy Owen, AB, MN, Second World War
Hugh T. Owen, Mona Terrace
Lewis Owen
Capt. Richard Owen, Augusta Place
Robert William Owen, Halfway House
Capt. Owen Owens, Halfway House, *ob.* 28.10.1892, 60
Walter Palmer, SS *Elidir*, *ob.* 20.04.1993, 96
Capt. Hugh David Parry, Quay House, *Juliet Duff*, *ob.* 1968, 61
Capt. Owen Parry, *ob.* 18.05.1879, 62
Capt. Rice Parry, Angorfa, *ob.* 16.08.1911
Capt. Richard Parry, Mona Terrace, *ob.* 31.07.1915, 89
Capt. Robert Parry, SS *Alliance*, 20 Bangor Street, *ob.* 4.06.1898, 58
Robert William Parry, RN, HMS *Defence*, *ob.* 31.05.1916, 26
Capt. Thomas Henry Parry, *ob.* 1912, 58
Thomas John Parry
Capt. William Parry, Port Terrace, *Menai*, *ob.* 15.10.1874, 52
William Parry, Bryn Ffynnon Road, *ob.* 2.05.1915, 57
Capt. William Parry, Brynffynnon, *Catherine*, *ob.* 31.10.1905, 78
David Pierce, Boston Terrace, RMS *Loanda*, *ob.* 30.06.1895, 43

Henry R. Pierce, Trinity pilot, 33 Beach Road, *ob.* 6.05.1918, 48
John Pierce *ob.* 13.04.1874, 21
John Pierce, 33 Beach Road, *ob.* 15.11.1907, 82
Richard Pierce, *ob.* 27.09.1887, 27
Richard Pierce, Dinas
Capt. Robert Pierce, 22 Bangor Street
William Pierce, 20 Beach Road
John L. Pritchard, *Annie*, *ob.* 27.10.1892, 19
Llywelyn Prichard, RNR, First World War
Capt. David Pugh, Menai Street, *ob.* 29.06.1893, 69
Capt. Edward Pugh, *ob.* 14.01.1864, 34
Capt. Joseph Richardson, *ob.* 1885, 59
Capt. David Roberts, 15 Terfyn Terrace, *ob.* 6.04.1941, 72
Capt. Edward Roberts, Treflys, *ob.* 3.01.1944, 64
Evan Roberts, 4 Terfyn Terrace, *ob.* 1883, 15
Capt. Evan Roberts, Snowdon Street, *ob.* 21.11.1879, 33
Capt. Griffith Roberts, 4 Terfyn Terrace, *ob.* 8.11.1903, 79
John Roberts, Pilot, *ob.* 1892, 77
Capt. John Roberts, *Antelope*, *ob.* 15.01.1913, 74
Capt. John Roberts, 9 Port Terrace, *ob.* 11.12.1914, 57
Capt. John Roberts, 59 Bangor Street
J.O. Roberts, Efrog House, Bangor Street, Bangor
John Robert Roberts, Bryn Alun, RN, First World War
Capt. Owen Roberts, Menai Street, *ob.* 6.04.1898, 78
Capt. Richard Ellis Roberts, *ob.* 13.03.1883, 49
Robert Roberts, *ob.* 9.05.1851, 42
Capt. Robert Roberts, *ob.* 25.07.1851, 47
Capt. Robert Roberts, Mona View, *ob.* 24.07.1900, 38
Capt. Robert Ellis Roberts, *ob.* 13.03.1885, 49
Thomas Roberts, Menai Street, *Annie*, *ob.* 27.10.1892
Capt. Thomas Wilson Roberts, Bodawel, *ob.* 1937, 80
Capt. William Roberts, *Margaret & Martha*, *ob.* 11.09.1871, 66
Capt. William Roberts, *Edward Beck*, *ob.* 16.05.1876, 42
Capt. William Roberts, 4 Terfyn Terrace, *ob.* 1883, 30
Capt. William Roberts, *Ocean Maid*, *ob.* 16.01.1894, 67
Ellis Thomas, Tyn-y-Cae, *ob.* 19.06.1897, 65
Capt Henry Thomas, Awelfryn, *ob.* 10.10.1933, 74
Capt. John Thomas, Estate Yard Cottage, *ob.* 24.02.1911, 40
Capt. Joseph Thomas, Menai Street, *ob.* 1873, 45
Capt. Robert David Thomas, died.09.1914
Capt. Robert David Thomas, Menai Street, *ob.* 2.04.1930, 44
Thomas Thomas, Pilot, *ob.* 1879, 80
Capt. William Thomas, 1 Menai Street, *Galloway Lass*, *ob.* 3.06.1875, 43
Capt. John Joseph Tildsley, MN, Bryn Melyn, *ob.* 1959, 88
Capt. Ben Williams, Hafan *ob.* 1952, 76

Capt Hugh D. Parry.
[Yvonne Edwards]

Capt. Robert Pierce.

Capt. Thomas W. Roberts.

Capt Ben Williams
[Margaret Tuzuner].

Capt. John Williams
[SS Alistair*].*

Capt. Robert Williams,
Bangor Street.
[Margaret Tuzuner]

Capt. D.G. Williams, Halfway, *ob.* 5.04.1986, 80

Capt. Evan Williams, brig *Ellinor*, *ob.* 19.04.1831, 26

Glynn George Williams, RN, *ob.* 1981, 82

Capt. Griffith Williams, *Catherine Roberts*, *ob.* 13.08.1888, 54

Petty Officer Gwilym Williams, RN

Capt. Hugh Williams, *Cambrian Queen*, *ob.* 20.03.1894, 35

Capt. Hugh Williams, Caegwyndryn, *ob.* 24.12.1913, 56

John Williams, Monfa, MN, *Connemara*, *ob.* 3.11.1916, 22

Capt. John Williams, 15 Florence Terrace, *ob.* 3.01.1890, 51

Capt. John Williams, Helen Terrace, *Cambria*, *ob.* 12.03.1907, 56

Capt. John Williams, SS *Alistair*, *ob.* 20.12.1907, 53

John Williams, 18 Menai Street, *ob.* 5.03.1909, 54

Lewis Williams, *ob.* 8.09.1917, 64

Owen Williams, *ob.* 3.03.1888, 47

Owen Williams, *ob.* 31.05.1888, 21

Capt. Owen Williams, 10 Bangor Street, *ob.* 22.07.1894, 29

Capt. Owen Williams, 5 Sea View Terrace, SS *Monarch*, *ob.* 1908, 35

PO Owen Williams, MN, Second World War

Capt. Owen Williams, Ferndale, *ob.* 23.03.1928

Owen Glyn Williams, 30 Bangor Street

Owen Lewis Williams, *ob.* 4.08.1891, 20

Richard Williams, Menai Stores

Capt. Robert Williams, Augusta Place, *ob.* 16.02.1876, 38

Robert Williams, 5 Sea View Terrace, *Annie*, *ob.* 27.10.1892, 13

Capt. Robert Williams, 30 Bangor Street

Robert Arthur Williams, 30 Bangor Street

Thomas J. Williams, 8 Snowdon Street, *ob.* 1941, 34

Capt. Thomas O. Williams, MN, 14 Helen Terrace, *ob.* 6.03.1942, 65

William Williams, *ob.* 15.08.1861, 25

William Williams, RN, 5 Sea View, First World War

William Williams, 2 Beach Road, *ob.* 23.12.1924, 74

Capt. William Williams, PS *Snowdon*, 1941

Capt. W Williams, Islwyn

Capt. William David Williams, SS *Velinheli*, *ob.* 1952, 47

William Grey Williams, RN, 30 Bangor Street,

William Pugh Williams, 23 Bangor Street, *ob.* 10.01.1929, 80

Other ships that Port Dinorwic men are known to have served on:

Alice – William Davies, AB, also *Bodicea*

Ann & Laura – William Jones, mate, also *William Bowden*

Becky Sharp – William Edwards, boy

Canadian – Robert Jones, AB, also *Peleus*

Ellen – Daniel Edwards, AB, also *Margaret*

– William Evans, master

– Henry Hughes, AB, also *William*

Fairy – John Lewis, AB, also *Amiable* 1881
 – Griffith Roberts, boy, also *Planet* 1881
 – Owen Roberts, boy, also *Penmaen* 1881
Gleaner – Capt. Hugh Roberts, 1876
Isabella – John Roberts, OS, also *Vaynol* 1893
Kate – Capt. Thomas Williams, also *Winifred* 1913
Lady Elizabeth – William Hughes, AB, also *Thauma* 1892
 – Thomas Williams, AB, also *North Cambria* 1892
Llanelly – David Owens, AB, also *Ninadria* 1892
Louis Napoleon – John Jones, mate, also *Eleanor Thomas*, 1873
 – John Roberts, AB, also *Eleanor Thomas* 1873
 – John Williams, OS, also *Eleanor Thomas* 1873
Louise – John Lewis, AB
Margaret & Mary – John Roberts, OS, also *Progress* 1874
Merle – Capt. Robert A. Roberts
Port Antonio – William Hughes, 2nd engineer
Pursuit – Capt. William Jones
 – Hugh Williams, OS and cook, also *Wepre Lass*
Queen Victoria – John Roberts, AB
Royal Charter – Edward Edwards, AB, also *Batavia*, 1873
Seven Brothers – W. Humphreys, mate, also *Eleanor and Jane*, 1876
Snaefell – Daniel Edwards, AB, also SS *Voltaic*
William – William Edwards, OS, also *Mary Rowlands*, 1875
 – William Edwards, OS, also *Elizabeth & Mary*, 1875
 – Edward Edwards, mate, also *Ellen*, 1875
 – Henry Jones, boy
 – Capt. Thomas Jones
 – William Jones, OS, also *Climax*, 1875
 – Robert Richards, mate, also *Progress*, 1875
 – Humphrey Williams, mate, also *William*
Xanthus – William Parry, also *Catharina*, 1882
 – Hugh Roberts, also *Mary Rowlands*, 1882

On their retirement from the sea, many of the captains were appointed harbour master at Port Dinorwic including: W.B. Buckingham; Robert Davies; W. Morris Elias; Thomas Griffith; Capt. William Griffith; John Hughes; Robert Hughes; Tom Pownall; Capt. Thomas Wilson Roberts; Capt. Ben Williams. The Rev. Morris Hughes, who had no prior maritime connection, also served as harbour master.

APPENDIX 2
WAR MEMORIAL

Meetings were held to discuss the most appropriate form that a memorial to honour those killed in the First World War should take and resulted in some favouring a memorial clock whilst others thought that a memorial hall would be more appropriate. Each project had its merits: the clock in the main street would be seen by everyone and would be a regular reminder of the sacrifices made, whereas others favoured a much needed public hall with a room within specially dedicated as a memorial. Those who had been in favour of building a memorial hall decided at a meeting held at the Conservative Club on 8 July 1921 to proceed with the project.

A site under consideration was that next to Assheton House shop (then used for storing coal and later occupied by the Central Garage), but the sum of £200 demanded for the remaining fifty-seven years of the lease was considered too high. Other sites were also considered, including the station field, the back of Bangor Street 'near Robert Williams's stable' and land between Bethania and Elim chapels. The council minutes recorded that 'if the hall was built then the YWCA (Young Women Christian Association) would make an application for the use of some rooms in the building and would contribute £300 if that was possible [sic].' The response, if any, is not recorded.

The Parish Council also recorded that a Hugh Lloyd Roberts, a native of Port Dinorwic who had emigrated to the USA and had become a resident in New York, had stated when visiting his family at Efrog House in 1923, that he was prepared to contribute the sum of £100 towards the purchase of land to enable a hall to be built. As soon as a site at the back of Bangor Street had been approved by the Vaynol estate agent and the land purchased, a letter was sent to Roberts requesting the sum of £100 and this was received in September 1923. Additionally a £1,000 legacy left by the late Mrs Thompson (of Terfyn Terrace) in 1901 towards a 'public hall' also assisted towards the costs.

The hall would be designed by Capt. T.E. Jones of Terfyn Terrace and built by contractors G. & J. Gregory of Caernarvon. During its construction, one wall was blown down in a severe gale and, even when the foundation stone was being laid by Sir Michael Duff on 31 October 1925, with the Llanrug Band in attendance, 'the proceedings were accompanied by thunder and lightning'.

Those who had been in favour of a memorial clock also decided to proceed with the project. It was designed by Mr Segar-Owen FRIBA and built by J.M. Jones of Amlwch in Anglesey granite on a site donated by the Vaynol estate and the directors of the London Midland & Scottish Railway Company, at the bottom of Station Hill in 1926.

The War Memorial Clock immediately prior to its unveiling in 1926. [Margaret Tuzuner].

In addition to the two memorials mentioned, a local newspaper reported:

Port Dinorwic Heroes – Memorial Tablet Unveiled – An interesting ceremony was witnessed at Port Dinorwic on Saturday when a memorial tablet to those who had made the supreme sacrifice in the Great War and who were members of the Port Dinorwic Conservative Club was unveiled by the Hon. Walter Warwick Vivian of Glyn, Bangor. The Conservative Club was packed to overflowing. The names on the Tablet were Robin Duff, Evan H. Williams, William H. Davies and Evan Jones, all killed in 1918 (Hon. Sec. of the Memorial Fund Griffith Ellis, Cae Glas, Port Dinorwic). [GAS C&DH 22 October 1920]

The Fallen – First World War

BUTLER, CHARLES HENRY, born Richmond, Surrey, husband of Mary (née Howells of Port Dinorwic), Frondeg. Acting second hand, 1307D, Royal Naval Reserve. He died whilst serving on HM Trawler *Morococala* which was sweeping for mines off Queenstown, Ireland, when she was struck by a mine launched from the UC-31, 9 November 1917. Aged 46. Portsmouth Naval Memorial.

DAVIES, DAVID BENJAMIN, son of William and Ellen I. Davies of Elm Cottage. Private, 265501, 1/6th Bn Royal Welsh Fusiliers, died 1 May 1917. Jerusalem War Cemetery, Israel.

DAVIES, RICHARD HOWEL, son of Robert and Margaret Davies, 7 Snowdon Street. Sapper, WR/505552, Royal Engineers (Inland Water Transport), died of shock, France, 7 September 1918, aged 37. Les Baraques Military Cemetery, Sangatte, France.

DAVIES, WILLIAM HENRY. Private, 25971, Royal Welsh Fusiliers, died 20 July 1916, aged 22. Llantysilio Churchyard, Llangollen.

DUFF, SIR ROBERT (ROBIN) GEORGE VIVIAN, (born London) son of Sir Charles Garden Assheton-Smith of Vaenol and husband of Lady Juliet Lowther Duff of Wilton. Lieutenant, 2nd Life Guards, died Langemark, Belgium, 16 October 1914, age 37. Cement House Cemetery, Langemark, Belgium.

ELLIS, JOHN. Petty officer, Royal Naval Volunteer Reserve.

GRIFFITH, HUGH, of 4 Bryn Afon, Tan-y-Maes. Private, 1520, Royal Welsh Fusiliers, died at Caernarfon Fever Hospital, 3 February 1922.

GRIFFITHS, EDWARD HUMPHREY, (born Liverpool) son of Lewis and Sarah Griffiths of 6 Snowdon Street. Private, 28595, 19th Bn Royal Welsh Fusiliers, killed in action, France, 6 June 1916, aged 24. Loos British Cemetery, France.

GRIFFITHS, JOHN ARTHUR, son of Hugh and Ann Griffiths, 4 Bryn Afon, Tan-y-Maes. Sapper, 6785, 2nd Siege Company (Royal Anglesey), Royal Engineers, killed in action, Ypres, 4 May 1916. Ypres Town Cemetery Extension, Belgium.

HUGHES, JOHN, 15 Brynffynnon Road. Private, 1542 & 265478, 1/6th (Carnarvonshire & Anglesey) Bn, Royal Welsh Fusiliers, died 10 August 1915. Helles Memorial, Gallipoli, Turkey.

HUGHES, JOHN EDWYN, BA, son of Edward and Mary Hughes, of 27 Augusta Place and husband of Sydney Ellen (née Williams) of Stag Cottage, Llanfairpwll. Lieutenant, 10th Bn Royal Welsh Fusiliers, killed in action 19 August 1916, age 29. Dive Copse, British Cemetery Sailly-Le-Sac, Somme, France.

HUGHES, OWEN, born Bodorgan, son of Owen and Margaret Hughes and husband of Elizabeth of 15 Brynffynnon Road. Private, 1844 1/6th Royal Welsh Fusiliers, died of dysentery, Egypt, 5 May 1916, aged 44. Cairo War Memorial Cemetery, Egypt.

HUMPHREYS, HUGH GRIFFITH, son of William and Ellen Humphreys, 8 Augusta Place. Private, 42120, 12th Bn Suffolk Regiment, died of wounds whilst a prisoner of war in Germany, 6 May 1918. Cologne Southern Cemetery, Germany.

JONES, DAVID, born Llandeiniolen, husband of Kate Jones, 27 Bush Road. Stoker, V547, trawler HMS Flicker, Royal Naval Reserve, died 4 March 1916, aged 43, as the result of his ship being mined while on patrol duty off Admiralty Pier, Dover.

JONES, EVAN, son of Evan and Ellen Jones of 27 Brynffynnon Road and husband of Elizabeth Jones, Library House, Bala. Private, 47462, 9th Bn Welsh Regiment, killed in action, Belgium, 29 April 1918, aged 42. Tyne Cot Memorial, Belgium.

JONES, HUGH EMRYS, son of Hugh and Jane E. Jones, 19 Augusta Place. Private, 36833, 184th Company, Machine Gun Corps (Infantry), killed in action, France, 26 August 1916, aged 18. Laventie Military Cemetery, La Gorgue, France.

JONES, OWEN ARTHUR, son of Captain and Mrs M.E. Jones of Assheton House. Private, 38509, 2/5th Bn Gloucestershire Regiment, killed in action, France, 20 October 1918, aged 21. Romeries Communal Cemetery Extension, France.

JONES, OWEN CECIL, son of surgeon Owen Jones and Catherine Ann of Terfyn Terrace. Major, 1/7th Bn Royal Welsh Fusiliers, died of wounds 30 December 1917, aged 34. Jerusalem War Cemetery, Israel.

JONES, ROBERT RICHARD, son of Sam and Mary Jones of Winnipeg. Private, 460324, Royal Canadian Regiment, died 4 October 1916, aged 21. Contay British Cemetery, Contay, France.

JONES, WILLIAM BARTHOLOMEW, son of surgeon Owen Jones and Catherine Ann of Terfyn Terrace. Second lieutenant, 134th Bn Machine Gun Corps (Infantry), missing (believed killed), France, 27 May 1918, aged 35. Soissons Memorial, Aisne, France.

JONES, REV. WILLIAM EVANS, Baptist minister, son of Eliza Evans Jones, Roewen Cottages. Captain (chaplain 4th class), Army Chaplain's Department, attached 2nd Bn Royal Welsh Fusiliers, killed 8 October 1918, aged 24. Prospect Hill Cemetery, Gouy, France.

JONES, WILLIAM RICHARD, 9 Augusta Place. Seaman, SS *Braeglen*, Merchant Marine, drowned in Liverpool Bay, 2 August 1916, following a collision with SS *Sarah Brough*. The *Braeglen* was sailing from Llanddulas to Ayr carrying gravel. Eight of the eleven crew were lost.

LLOYD, WILLIAM, Crûg. Private, L/10454, 7th Bn Royal Sussex Regiment, killed in action, France, 9 April 1917. Arras Memorial, France.

MORGAN, THOMAS, son of Thomas and Margaret Morgan, Glan-yr-Afon, Tregarth. Private, 1677, D Company, 1/10th Bn Manchester Regiment, died Gallipoli, 4 June 1915, aged 20, Helles Memorial, Gallipoli, Turkey.

OWEN, HUGH, son of Hugh and Mary Owen of Rhydd-Dîr, Griffith's Crossing. Private, 56934, 3rd Bn Royal Welsh Fusiliers transferred to 550th Agricultural Company, Labour Corps, died of wounds 7 November 1918, aged 27. Llanfairisgaer Churchyard.

OWEN, JOHN, MM, born Cader Elwg, Port Dinorwic, son of Robert and Margaret Owen of Bryn Kenrick, Llanfairtalhaiarn. Sapper, 154420, Depot, Special Brigade, Royal Engineers, died 11 December 1917, aged 27. Llanddeiniolen Cemetery.

OWEN, RICHARD HUGH, son of John and Ellen Owen of 29 Beach Road and husband of Ellen (née Roberts) of 62 Beach Road, Bangor, New South Wales, former mariner and labourer, 7807. Private, 35th Bn Australian Imperial Force (enlisted 10 October 1917, Sydney, New South Wales, arrived Liverpool 20 April 1918), gun-shot wound in abdomen 22 August 1918, died of wounds, France, 22 August 1918, aged 39. Daours Communal Cemetery Extension, France.

OWEN, RICHARD JONES, 18 Tan-y-Maes. Private, 34446, 1st Bn King's (Liverpool) Regiment, missing (believed killed), France, 27 December 1917. Arras Memorial, France.

OWEN, WILLIAM HENRY, son of Hugh and Mary Owen of Tyddyn Hen, Bethel Road, Caernarfon, formerly of Rhydd Dîr. Lance corporal, 36838, 61st Company, Machine Gun Corps, died of wounds, France 26 August 1917, aged 22. Etaples Military Cemetery, France.

PARRY, ROBERT WILLIAM, son of Owen and Margaret Parry of 8 Brynffynnon Road. Acting leading stoker, K15305, cruiser HMS *Defence*, killed in action at the Battle of Jutland, 31 May 1916, aged 25. Plymouth Naval Memorial.

PEARSON, WALTER PHILISON, son of Walter Henry and A.E. Pearson of Aber Cottage. Bugler, 13250, King's Royal Rifle Corps, died 19 August 1918. His official age was given as 16, but he was actually born in 1902. Ripon Cemetery.

PRITCHARD, HUGH, son of Hugh Pritchard, 20 Menai Street and husband of L. Pritchard, Manchester House, Nant-y-Moel, Bridgend. Private 290977, 1/1st Monmouthshire Regiment, killed in action, France, 27 October 1917. Philisophe British Cemetery, Mazingarbe, France.

PRITCHARD, LLEWELYN, son of Thomas and Jane Pritchard of Aber Cottages. Stoker, 7976S, Royal Naval

Reserve, HM Transport *Royal Edward*, torpedoed by UB-14 off Kandeloussa, Greece, died 13 August 1915, aged 34. Portsmouth Naval Memorial.

ROBERTS, EDWARD, son of William and Grace Roberts, 3 Sea View Terrace. Private, 33213, 3rd Bn Cheshire Regiment, died of wounds, France, 24 October 1916, aged 22. Etaples Military Cemetery, France.

ROBERTS, HUGH, son of Mrs M. Roberts, 23 Menai Street. Private, 8992, 3/4th Bn, Royal Welsh Fusiliers, died 16 June 1916. Llanfairisgaer Churchyard.

ROBERTS, JOHN, son of Captain John and Catherine Jane Roberts, 59 Bangor Street. Private, 487337, 1st Canadian Pioneers, died of sickness in Canada, 18 November 1916, aged 45. Kamloops (Pleasant Street) Cemetery, British Columbia.

ROBERTS, THOMAS, son of William Roberts, 16 Carnarvon Road. Private, 54967, Royal Welsh Fusiliers, died of wounds, 27 October 1918 whilst a prisoner of war, aged 34. Liege (Robermont) Cemetery, Belgium.

STEVENSON, KENELM JULIAN, son of Richard R. and Amy F. Stevenson of London and husband of E. Stevenson of Islington, London, lived at 2 Port Terrace. Private, 23258, 16th Bn Royal Welsh Fusiliers, died of wounds, France, 26 August 1918, aged 40. Daours Communal Cemetery Extension, Somme, France.

WILLIAMS, EVAN HUGH, 23 Bangor Street. Lance corporal, 8977, 2nd Bn Manchester Regiment, killed in action, France, 3 June 1918. Cabaret-Rouge British Cemetery, Souchez, France.

WILLIAMS, JOHN, 22 Beach Road. Private, 291375, 1/7th Royal Welsh Fusiliers, killed in action in Palestine, 29 December 1917. Jerusalem War Cemetery, Israel.

WILLIAMS, JOHN. Mercantile Marine.

WILLIAMS, RICHARD, husband of Maggie Tate (formerly Williams) 37 Carnarvon Road. Private, 54673, 16th Bn Royal Welsh Fusiliers, killed in action, 26 August 1918, aged 25. Vis-en-Artois Memorial, France.

WILLIAMS, ROBERT, son of Thomas Williams, 2 Glanffynnon, Tan-y-Maes. Private, 30416, 4th Bn 3rd New Zealand Rifle Brigade, killed in action, Belgium, 7 June 1917. Messines Ridge (New Zealand) Memorial, Belgium.

WILLIAMS, ROBERT HUGHES, 67 Bangor Street. Private, 35850, 20th (Labour) Bn, Cheshire Regiment, died of gas poisoning in Bangor Hospital, 16 June 1919. Llanfairisgaer Churchyard.

WILLIAMS, THOMAS, son of William and Mary Ellen Williams of 22 Beach Road. Able seaman, 1811, Hood Bn, Royal Naval Division, died of wounds France, 25 February 1918, aged 20. St Pierre Cemetery, Amiens, France.

WILLIAMS, WILLIAM, 14 Beach Road. Sergeant, A2236115, Royal Garrison Artillery, died at home 15 September 1922 as the result of gas poisoning.

The Fallen – Second World War

BOWLES, CHARLES JAMES, husband of Elizabeth. Chief engineer officer, Merchant Navy, died 12 November 1941, age 64, when the MV *Maurita* was mined off Hilbre Swash in the Dee estuary whilst carrying 240 tons of coal from Point of Ayr to Lancaster. All five members of the crew were lost. Tower Hill Memorial.

CHUBB, SIDNEY MONS, born 1915, Port Dinorwic, son of Samuel Chubb (seaman, born Plymouth) and Elizabeth Jane (née Morris, born Port Dinorwic). Able seaman, Merchant Navy, 10 October 1942, aged 27. Llanfairisgaer Churchyard.

DAVIES, JOHN. Engineer, Merchant Navy.

ELLIS, WILLIAM, son of Robert and Jane Ellis and husband of Elizabeth. Chief officer, SS *Dalegarth Force*, Merchant Navy, died 22 March 1942 aged 63. Tower Hill Memorial, London.

EVANS, ROBERT MYRDDIN, son of Evan Price and Jennie Pugh Evans and husband of Mair. Sergeant, T/199120, 53 Infantry Brigade Group Company, Royal Army Service Corps, died 5 January 1944, aged 31. Thanbyuzayat War Cemetery, Myanmar (Burma).

FAVRETTO, WILLIAM, born Liverpool, son of Mark (born Austria) and Mary Ann (née Hughes of Port Dinorwic) Favretto, husband of Mary of 11 Port Terrace. Chief engineer, Merchant Navy, 16 March 1941, aged 51.

HUGHES, HERBERT ELLIS, son of Captain William and Margaret Hughes, husband of Elizabeth Catherine. Chief officer, Merchant Navy, SS *Pamela* (owned by Anglesey Shipping Company, Port Penrhyn) which was lost with all hands in transit from Sharpness to Belfast laden with barley (but had been diverted to Liverpool) most probably as a result of striking a drifting mine in the Irish Sea somewhere south west of Anglesey, 11 October 1944. Aged 44. Tower Hill Memorial, London.

HUGHES, RICHARD, son of Elizabeth Hughes of Bangor. Fireman, Merchant Navy, SS *King Gruffydd*. He was one of 24 crew members who died when the ship sank midway across the North Atlantic after being attacked by U-338 at 03.05 hours on 17 March 1943, en route from New York to Loch Ewe and Hull, whilst part of convoy SC-122. Aged 28. Tower Hill Memorial.

JENNINGS, WILLIAM GLYNNE, son of Joseph and Jennie (née Roberts) Jennings. Blacksmith 5th class, D/MX74457, battlecruiser HMS *Repulse*, Royal Navy, one of 508 crew who died when the ship was sunk by Japanese torpedo bombers off Malaya, 10 December 1941. Aged 20. Plymouth Naval Memorial.

JONES, JOHN MORRIS, son of Hugh and Jane Ellen Jones. Able seaman, Merchant Navy, SS *Andora Star*, died 2 July 1940, aged 49, when ship was torpedoed off the coast of Ireland by U-47 when en route from Liverpool to St John's carrying 1200 German and Italian internees. Tower Hill Memorial.

JONES, THOMAS WILLIAM, son of William Llewelyn and Ellinor Jones. Driver, T/14432236, Royal Army Service Corps, died 31 May 1944, aged 18. Worcester (Astwood) Cemetery.

LLOYD-JONES, THOMAS HENRY, son of Llewelyn and Eva Mary Lloyd-Jones. Lieutenant, Royal Naval Volunteer Reserve, died 24 February 1945, age 35, when HM Trawler *Ellesmere* was sunk by U-1203 south of Penzance Bay. Lowestoft Naval Memorial.

McGUIRE, WILLIAM RICHARD. Fireman, Merchant Navy.

OWEN, EMLYN, son of Thomas and Elizabeth Owen, husband of Elizabeth of Llandwrog. Able seaman, Merchant Navy, died 3 February 1943, aged 23, when MV *Inverilen*, an oil tanker en route from New York to Stanlow, was torpedoed and sunk by U-456. Tower Hill Memorial.

OWEN, GORONWY, son of Mr and Mrs H. Owen. Able seaman, Merchant Navy, died 26 March 1941, aged 28, when SS *Brier Rose* was lost with all hands from 'War Causes' in the Irish Sea whilst sailing to Cardiff from Belfast laden with steel billets. Tower Hill Memorial.

PARRY, WILLIAM, son of Robert and Mary Parry. Stoker 2nd class, Royal Navy, P/KX126636, killed 25

November 1941, aged 25, when the battleship HMS *Barham* was sunk by U-331 in the Mediterranean north of Sidi Barrani, Egypt; 841 of her crew were lost. Portsmouth Naval Memorial.

ROBERTS, ROBERT BADEN POWELL, son of William J. and Catherine Roberts, Aber Cottages, and husband of Elizabeth Annie, driver, 159558, 179th Field Ambulance, Royal Army Ordinance Corps, died 30 October 1940, aged 40. Llanfairisgaer Churchyard.

WILLIAMS, OWEN. Petty officer, Merchant Navy.

WILLIAMS, THOMAS OWEN. Master mariner.

The CWGC slate headstone to
Pte Hugh Owen
Royal Welsh Fusiliers
in Llanfairisgaer Churchyard. (AC)

APPENDIX 3
SHOPS

Shops c.1905-1910 as from Terfyn Terrace:

Corner of Terfyn Terrace and Port Terrace, John Owen, selling exotic foods including cheeses, salami, German sausages, spices and olives (the property was purchased by Lloyds Bank *c*.1907).

Berw House (corner of Terfyn Terrace and Port Terrace) kept by the tailor Owen Morgan .

14 Bangor Street, Fron Heulog, temperance hotel and café kept by Misses Alice and Nell Thomas.

22 Bangor Street, Thomas Roberts, painter and plumber, later Dr ap Vychan Jones's surgery.

24 Bangor Street, William P. Owen, bootmaker and shoe repairer.

26 Bangor Street, Revere House, stationer and newspapers.

28 Bangor Street, original Conservative Club, later Hugh Jones, butcher.

32 Bangor Street, Manchester House, J.V. Williams, draper and grocer.

51 Bangor Street, Post Office, sub-postmaster R.C. Griffith.

53 Bangor Street, R.C. Griffith chemist, followed by G.H. Jones, chemist.

54 Bangor Street, Windsor House, Mrs E. Griffiths, boot and shoe shop, followed by John Rowlands, tailor.

55 Bangor Street, Dinorwic House, David Evans, grocer, later J. Henry Jones and family.

57 Bangor Street, Paris House, Hannah Parry, fresh fish shop, later Mrs Jones (Bodwyn), sweets.

65 Bangor Street, Clynnog House, Mrs M. Jones, confectioner.

67 Bangor Street, Henry Bank (son of H.M. Bank), cycle and watch repairer, later Trevor Williams, Post Office.

69 Bangor Street, Bryn Morfydd, William Jones, baker, later Gwyrfai Jones, chemist.

71 Bangor Street, Greenwich House, H.M. Bank, jeweller and cycle dealer, later the YMCA.

73 Bangor Street, W. Caddock, tea rooms, later Mr & Mrs William Roberts, groceries.

74 J. Thomas, tailor.

75 Bangor Street, T. Francis, barber (previously occupied Mona House, Snowdon Street, barber and taxidermist).

76 Bangor Street, London House, Eiffel Café and commercial hotel kept by Miss Williams and her brother, Robert, who also had a horse and trap for local use.

78 Bangor Street, William Schow, greengrocer.

Victoria Hotel, Charles Roberts.

82 Bangor Street, Edmund Jones, pork butcher.

Miss Jones, dressmaker.

84 Bangor Street, John Henry Jones, monumental mason, stationer, photographer and printer.

88 Bangor Street, Menai Stores, Richard Williams, grocer.

89 & 90 Bangor Street, John Jones, butcher, later Thomas Roberts (of Roberts & Sons), butcher.

Bangor House, 91 Bangor Street, Mrs H. Williams, grocer.

92 Bangor Street (previously Britannia Vaults) – W. Barnett, butcher.

Menai Hill, Miss Lloyd's sweet shop, later Elizabeth Edwards and her brother, Richard.

Menai Hill, Griffith Jones, coal merchant (yard adjoined the railway bridge).

93 Bangor Street, Vaynol House, Mrs Morgan, second-hand clothing.

Springfield, Hugh Evans, draper, woollen goods and yarn.

Augusta Place, Miss Williams, wool shop.

Mona House, Mrs E. Owen, grocer.

Maelog House, Mrs Rowlands, grocer.

Leicester House, John Thomas, shoe and boot maker.

Margaret A. Morrison, baker and confectioner.

Anchor House, Mrs Griffiths, milk, butter and eggs.

Snowdon Street, John Edwards, grocer.

Gwalia House, 8 Snowdon Street, J. & R. Williams, tailor.

10 Snowdon Street, Henry Lewis, cobbler, bootmaker.

Menai Street, Mr Hughes, baker.

Cinallt, Snowdon Street, Edward Edwards, grocer.

Bee Hive, Snowdon Street, Edward Parry, grocer.

Birmingham House, Snowdon Street, Henry Jones, glass and china ware.

Snowdon Street, Mrs Jane Hughes, greengrocer.

Snowdon Street, Mrs Theophilus Jones, grocer (now part of the Garddfon Inn).

Garddfon Inn, John Davies.

Beach Road, Ann Dop, sweets and cigarettes.

Beach Road, Michael Williams, blacksmith.

Beach Road, R. Lloyd, coal merchant.

Beach Road, Lewis Williams, chandlery.

Beach Road, R. Vaughan, fish fryer.

On the opposite side of the road from Aberpwll:
Rhiwal (Four Crosses), Mr Pritchard, general store.

Halfway House Inn (shop), items sold included jams, marmalade, pickles, sardines, lobster, tinned goods together with coffee and tea.

Florence House, 15 Bangor Street, grocer.

Central Garage, Bangor Street. Before this garage was built, this was the site of a coal yard.
[Len Williams]

Bangor Street, W.P. Williams, painter, wallpapers and paints, later Roger Williams, painter and decorator.

Railway House, 26 Bangor Street, Owen Roberts, butcher.

Arvonia, Bangor Street, William Jones, ironmonger, furniture, builders merchant, chandlery and agricultural implements.

60 Bangor Street, Griffith Williams, crockery and toys, later W. Horlocks fish and chips.

62 Bangor Street, Mrs Williams, sweets and groceries.

64 and 66 Bangor Street, space used as a coal yard, later a garage.

68 Bangor Street, Assheton House, Mr Bassett, general provisions.

72 Bangor Street, Vodol House, Richard Pritchard, draper.

77 Bangor Street, Drug Stores, O.R. Williams, general grocer, perfumes and soaps.

83 Bangor Street, Waterloo House, W. Ellis Thomas, master tailor.

85 Bangor Street, William Jones, tinplate and ironworker.

87 Bangor Street, Efrog House, John O. Roberts had a coal yard next to the house before it was converted into a garage where he kept a hansom cab and later an American Page car that he used for his taxi service.

Fron Dirion, Caernarfon Road, Mrs Davies, coal merchant.

Caernarfon Road, Mrs Williams, café.

Between Caernarfon Road and Dinas, Mrs Roberts, café, cigarettes, etc.

Caernarfon Road, Mrs Thomas (tŷ popty), bake house.

Llanfair House, Caernarfon Road, William Williams, grocer.

Brynffynnon Road, Miss Evans, sweets, cigarettes, grocer.

'Siop fawr', Boston Terrace, William Owen, grocer.

Menai View, Mrs Roberts, drapery and haberdashery.

Brynffynnon Road, Mrs E. Thomas, bakery and confectionery.

Cambria Model Bakery, John William, baker.

Libart yr Uchod, E. Jones, boot and shoe repairs.

Helen Terrace, Miss Jones, grocer.

Helen Terrace, Robert Williams, general store.

HALFWAY HOUSE INN LICENSEES

1825	Richard Jones (died 25 September 1825 aged 79); Margaret Jones (his wife died 23 July 1827 aged 81).
1827	John Roberts (died 30 July 1833).
1828	Extension built (cost £195 1s 4d).
1834	Elizabeth Roberts (died 13 September 1859).
1860	Margaret Jones.
1865	Owen Owens married Margaret Jones 18 July (ages 33 & 26).
1892	Owen Owens (died 28 October).
1892	Indenture: Margaret Owens, 12 November 1892.
1909	Agreement: Margaret Owen and Robert William Owen, 3 February.
1910	Billiard licence, Robert William Owen.
1917	Margaret Owen (died 15 July aged 77).
1931	Robert William Owen (died 12 March 1931 aged 61).
1931	Margaret Ann Owen (née Drummond) (died 11 March 1944 aged 67).
1944	David Glyn and Ethel (Effie) Williams (née Drummond, daughter of Margaret Ann Owen). After the death of his wife in 1968, D.G. Williams ran the Halfway for a few years before selling it to Ind Coope. He died on 5 April 1986.

Margaret Jane Jones.

Margaret Ann Owens.

Margaret Owen.

APPENDIX 5
POST OFFICE PERSONNEL

Rev. G.G. Owen.
[Kathleen Roberts]

Sub-postmasters:

    John Jones (9 August 1849–69)

    Richard Cadwaladr Griffith, MPS (1869–1905)

    Griffith Owen

    Rev. Griffith Gwynant Owen (1912–19)

    Robert Owen, 1919–45 (Mrs Mary Owen took over as deputy postmistress latterly)

    Trevor Williams (1945–18 August 1987)

Postmen and messengers:

    Griffith Jones, postman

    Thomas Roberts, messenger (1867)

    Edmund Jones, messenger (1871)

    Thomas Bradley, postman (August 1899)

    Edward Jones, postman

    John Alfonso Bank, postman (April 1900)

    Richard Edwards, postman

    Margaret Ellen Rowlands (1930s–40s)

    Richard Williams, postman

    Hughie Jones, postman

    Glyn G. Williams, postman (21 May 1937 – served for twenty-nine years)

    William Victor Williams, postman (served for twenty-five years)

Robert Owen.
[Kathleen Roberts]

John A. Bank.
[J. Heber Owen]

Hughie Jones (postman) with Mrs Mary Owen (deputy postmistress).
[Kathleen Roberts]

Select Bibliography

Published sources

Albert, William, *The Turnpike Road System in England*, CUP, 1972.

Bauglan, Peter E., *The Chester & Holyhead Railway*, David & Charles, 1972.

Borrow, George, *Wild Wales*, Bridge Books, 2009.

Boyd, James I.C., *Narrow Gauge Railways in North Caernarvonshire*, Oakwood Press, 1981.

Davies, H.R., *Conway and the Menai Ferries*, UWP, 1942.

Dodd, A.H., *The Industrial Revolution in North Wales*, Bridge Books, 1990.

Dodd, A.H., *A History of Caernarvonshire, 1284–1900*, Bridge Books, 1990.

Fenton, Richard, *Tours in Wales, 1802–13*, Hon. Society of Cymmrodorion, 1917.

Jones, R. Merfyn, *The North Wales Quarrymen, 1874–1922*, UWP, 1982.

Jones, Reg Chambers, *Dinorwic, the Llanberis Slate Quarry, 1780–1969*, Bridge Books, 2006.

Jones, Reg Chambers, *Sailing the Strait, aspects of Port Dinorwic and the Menai Strait*, Bridge Books, 2004.

Jones, Reg Chambers, *Crossing the Menai, an illustrated history of the ferries and bridges of the Menai Strait*, Bridge Books, 2011.

Jones, Reg Chambers, *Anglesey & Gwynedd, the War Years, 1939–45*, Bridge Books, 2008.

Rear, W.G., *LMS Branch Lines in North Wales*, Wild Swan Publications, 1986.

Thornley, F.C., *Steamers of North Wales*, Gwynedd Archives Service, n.d.

Williams, Gareth Haulfryn, *Railways in Gwynedd*, Gwynedd Archives Service, 1979.

Williams, John, *Hanes yr Achos yn Tanymaes ac Brynmenai*, n.d.

Journals and newspapers

Anglesey Antiquarian Scoiety Transactions
Caernarvon & Denbigh Herald
Caernarvonshire Historical Society Transactions
North Wales Chronicle
North Wales Gazette
Slaters Business Directory (various)